Report of the Chief Inspector of Marine Accidents

into the engine failure and subsequent

grounding of the Motor Tanker

BRAER

at Garths Ness, Shetland

on 5 January 1993

Marine Accident Investigation Branch
5/7 Brunswick Place
SOUTHAMPTON
Hants SO1 2AN

© Crown copyright 1994
Applications for reproduction should be made to HMSO
First published 1994
Second Impression 1994

ISBN 0 11 551210 1

Marine Accident Investigation Branch
Department of Transport
5/7 Brunswick Place
Southampton
Hants SO1 2AN

9 December 1993

The Right Honourable John MacGregor OBE MP
Secretary of State for Transport

Sir

In pursuance of Regulation 9 of the Merchant Shipping (Accident Investigation) Regulations 1989, I submit my Report following the Inspector's Inquiry into the engine failure and subsequent grounding of the motor tanker BRAER at Garths Ness, Shetland, on 5 January 1993.

I wish to place on record appreciation for the co-operation which was extended to the Inspectors who carried out the Inquiry, by the parties concerned.

The Inquiry was limited to investigating the causes of the engine failure and the actions which were taken both on board the vessel and ashore up to the time that the vessel went aground. It has not covered the pollution aspects of the accident as this is outside the remit of the Marine Accident Investigation Branch. However, the Marine Pollution Control Unit of the Department have carried out a review of the clean-up operation, and the Secretary of State for Scotland established an Ecological Steering Group to assess the impact of the spill on the natural environment of Shetland.

Also a separate and independent Inquiry has been commissioned by the Government to advise on whether any further measures are appropriate and feasible to protect the UK coastline from pollution from merchant shipping. The Inquiry is chaired by The Right Honourable The Lord Donaldson of Lymington, and the Report of the Inquiry is awaited.

I am, Sir,
Your obedient servant

Captain P B Marriott
Chief Inspector of Marine Accidents

CONTENTS

Page

1. SUMMARY

The motor tanker BRAER loaded with a full cargo of 84,700 tonnes of light crude oil sailed from Mongstad, Norway on 3 January 1993 for Quebec. The planned route would take the vessel through the North Fair Isle Strait towards Canada. Adverse weather was experienced as soon as BRAER cleared Mongstad and for the whole passage there were severe southerly gales. On the morning of 4 January four spare steel pipe sections, which had been secured on the port side of the after deck, broke loose and were rolling between the port side of the engine casing and the ship's port rails.

During the evening of 4 January, after routine adjustments to the auxiliary boiler, difficulty was experienced in re-igniting it. The auxiliary boiler provided steam for the necessary pre-heating of the heavy oil for the main engine and, pending the resumption of normal steam pressure, the main engine was changed from heavy oil to diesel oil.

Shortly after midnight, seawater contamination was discovered in the diesel oil supply line to the boiler and attempts were made to drain it. Some three hours later seawater contamination had also been discovered in the diesel oil service supply to the main engine and the generator. Attempts to drain the water from the diesel oil tanks continued, but at 0440 hrs the main engine stopped, followed by the failure of the generator.

The vessel was ten miles to the south of the Southern tip of Shetland and her Master advised the Coastguard of the loss of power and the vessel's position. BRAER was drifting to the north and her Master then requested towage assistance. Approximately two hours after stopping, BRAER had drifted to within four miles of Sumburgh Head and helicopter evacuation of non-essential crew was commenced. In the engine room, efforts to drain the water contamination and restore power continued. Tugs from Sullom Voe were already on the way and the tug/supply vessel STAR SIRIUS left Lerwick Harbour to go to BRAER's assistance. A further one and a half hours later BRAER was half a mile south-east of Horse Island and thought to be in imminent danger of grounding. The decision was made to abandon the vessel and the final evacuation of the crew was completed safely.

As the vessel then ceased to drift inshore it was decided to attempt to land volunteers on the forecastle head of BRAER to release her anchors. This plan had to be abandoned due to the proximity of the foremast, which precluded safe helicopter operations over the bow. STAR SIRIUS arrived on scene by which time BRAER was a mile south of Horse Island and drifting slowly to the west, influenced by the west going tidal stream. After passing Horse Island she again drifted to the north. Attempts were made to assemble a party, one of the volunteers of which was the Master of BRAER, with the aim of boarding the vessel at the stern and trying to set up a tow with STAR SIRIUS. The volunteers were landed on the stern and although a valiant attempt was made to take a messenger rope from STAR SIRIUS this failed and BRAER grounded on the west side of Garths Ness at 1119 hrs. The volunteers were safely evacuated.

1

The immediate cause of the accident was the contamination of the diesel oil supply by seawater entering the storage tanks from damaged air pipes. The damage was caused by one or more of the spare steel pipe sections which had broken loose in the severe weather conditions.

A number of recommendations are made which, if implemented, should prevent recurrence of such an accident in the future.

PART 1 FACTUAL ACCOUNT

2. PARTICULARS OF SHIP AND CREW

2.1 General Description

BRAER was a single-hulled crude oil carrier with the propelling machinery and accommodation superstructure in the conventional aft position. She was delivered as the HELLESPONT PRIDE, trading under that name until 1985 when she was sold and renamed BRAE TRADER. B+H (Bergvall & Hudner) bought the vessel in 1989 and changed the name to BRAER.

Port of Registry	:	Monrovia (Liberia)
Registered Owners	:	Braer Corporation, Monrovia
Managers	:	B+H Shipmanagement Co, Stamford, Ct, USA
Voyage Charterers	:	Canadian Ultramar Ltd, Montreal, Canada
Built	:	1975 Oshima Shipbuilding Co Ltd, Nagasaki, Japan
Length Overall	:	241.51m
Breadth Moulded	:	40.06m
Depth Moulded	:	18.80m
Gross Tonnage	:	44,989
Deadweight	:	89,730 tonnes
Loaded Draft	:	14.15m
Main Engine	:	Sumitomo-Sulzer Type 7RND90
Maximum Continuous Output	:	20,300 bhp at 122 rpm
Normal Output	:	18,270 bhp at 118 rpm
Electrical Generators	:	2 x 880 kW Diesel Driven
Auxiliary Boiler	:	1 Oil-Fired Water Tube Steam Pressure 16 Bar

Service Speed	:	14.5 Knots
Classification Society	:	Det Norske Veritas

The vessel was provided with a comprehensive range of navigational and communication equipment.

All the certificates for the vessel were in order and fully up-to-date.

2.2   **Management**

In 1989 BRAER was initially placed under the technical management of Singa Ship Management of Singapore, who also provided the crew manning for the vessel.   The technical management was transferred to B+H in July 1991, but crewing matters (except for the Master and certain non-Filipino senior officers) remained with Singa Ship Management AS of Oslo, who had taken over responsibility from their Singapore subsidiary in the previous year.

The B+H fleet of about 12 tankers is technically managed by engineer superintendents, formally titled Vessel Managers, each of whom is responsible for a section of the fleet. The Superintendent for BRAER had three other vessels within his responsibility and he reported to the Ship Manager at the B+H office in Stamford, USA. It was the practice of the Managers to place fitters on board their vessels as 'riding crews' on certain passages, in order to carry out routine maintenance and repair work while the vessel was at sea. Four Polish fitters had joined BRAER prior to her departure from her last port, Mongstad in Norway. The fitters worked under the direction of the Chief Engineer.

2.3   **Description of the Heavy Fuel Oil System**

The heavy fuel oil was stored in two wing deep tanks on the port and starboard sides, extending from the bottom shell to the upper deck, and a centre tank between No 1 platform deck and the upper deck. The total heavy fuel oil storage capacity was approximately 2,910 tonnes. In addition, two free-standing heavy fuel oil tanks were installed on No 1 platform deck, at the forward end of the engine room; one was the heavy fuel oil settling tank with a capacity of 47.4 tonnes and the other was the heavy fuel oil service tank with a capacity of 31.6 tonnes. On departure from Mongstad, on 3 January 1993, there was a total of 1,770 tonnes of heavy fuel oil on board.   On the basis of the engine averaging 106 revolutions per minute (rpm), the fuel consumption would have been approximately 52 tonnes per day.

Each heavy fuel oil wing deep tank was fitted with a forward and after air pipe, terminating on the upper deck just inboard of the ship's side. The centre heavy fuel oil tank was also fitted with two air pipes, one port and one starboard and also terminating on the upper deck, in way of the forward bulkhead of the engine casing. The heavy fuel oil settling and service tank air pipes joined into a common air pipe which terminated on the boat deck, on the starboard side. All the heavy fuel oil air pipes were fitted with float seal type heads 600mm above the deck.

The transfer of heavy fuel oil from any storage tank to the fuel oil settling and service tanks was via the heavy fuel oil transfer pump. This pump discharged into a common line feeding both the settling and service tanks, with isolation valves at the point of entry to each of those tanks, the one to the service tank normally being kept shut. Fuel oil from the settling tank was then continuously fed to one or both of the fuel oil purifiers and then to the fuel oil service tank. (The Inspectors were given to understand that the settling tank was continuously 'topped up' by use of an auto start facility on the transfer pump activated by a settling tank contents sensor, the suction valves from both wing deep tanks having been left open since the vessel departed from Mongstad).

2.4   **Description of the Diesel Oil System**

The diesel oil storage tanks were two double bottom tanks, port and starboard, sited beneath the engine room. They had a total capacity of approximately 297 tonnes. In addition there were two free standing diesel oil tanks on No 1 platform deck, near the forward end of the engine room on the starboard side; one was the settling tank and the other was the service tank, each having a capacity of approximately 11.5 tonnes. On departure from Mongstad there was a total of 126 tonnes of diesel fuel on board. Each diesel generator would consume approximately 4.7 tonnes per day at maximum output.

Each double bottom diesel tank was fitted with two air pipes, one forward and one aft, both terminating on the upper deck, just inboard of the ship's side. The diesel settling and service tank air pipes joined together within the engine space into a common air pipe, which terminated on the upper deck, on the starboard side adjacent to the accommodation bulkhead. All the diesel oil air pipes were fitted with float seal type heads.

Transfer of diesel oil from the double bottom storage tanks was via the diesel fuel oil transfer pump to a common line, feeding both the service and settling tanks, with an isolation valve at the point of entry to each tank. This operation was carried out under hand control, the transfer pump being started and stopped as necessary, although there was an auto stop level switch fitted to the diesel oil settling tank. Diesel oil was fed from the settling tank to the service tank through the diesel oil purifier.

(The Inspectors were given to understand that the diesel oil settling tank was 'topped up' every 12 hours by the 8 to 12 watchkeepers; similarly, the service tank was 'topped up' from the settling tank, through the purifiers, during the same period).

2.5   **Description of the Steam Generating Plant**

In common with many motor vessels built in the early 1970s, the design criteria for BRAER specified that whilst the generators would operate on diesel oil, the main engine should be capable of using the heavier and less expensive fuel oils. The Sulzer 7RND90 main engine was designed to operate on high viscosity or heavy fuel whilst at sea but on the lighter diesel fuel when manoeuvring or in restricted waters. Irrespective of the type of fuel used, efficient combustion requires that the correct atomising viscosity must be achieved at the engine fuel injectors.

In the case of the lighter diesel fuel, the viscosity is sufficiently low to enable this to be achieved without further treatment. For heavy fuel oil, heating is necessary to lower the viscosity to an acceptable level. On BRAER, this heating was achieved by the use of relatively low pressure steam generated from two sources: an oil fired auxiliary boiler and a main engine exhaust economiser. The main engine exhaust was permanently connected to the economiser unit; no exhaust gas by-pass valve was fitted.

The maximum steam output generated by the auxiliary boiler was 55,000 kgs per hour at the pressure of 16 Bar. The main fuel used was heavy fuel oil, with diesel oil used for a cold start or in an emergency. The exhaust gas economiser generated 1,800 kgs per hour at 9 Bar when the main engine was operating at its continuous service rating. The steam generating system on BRAER, although supplying primary steam at 16 Bar, also supplied two separate sub-systems, one at 9 Bar for various fuel oil heating requirements and another at 5 Bar for domestic and trace heating and other uses. These steam generating capacities were the designed outputs when the vessel was built. The capacity of both units at the time of departure from Mongstad would have been about 85% of those quoted above. The exhaust gas economiser was only capable of 'topping up' the steam supply during a period of heavy demand, most of the steam demand being supplied by the auxiliary boiler. The steam demand varies with the time of year and the ambient air and sea temperatures. In tropical zones the steam demand would have been low, when the exhaust gas economiser would have been capable of supplying the whole steam demand.

2.6 The Superintendent

The Superintendent joined the vessel at Mongstad. BRAER had recently been transferred to his group of vessels and he was on board to familiarise himself and prepare her for a forthcoming classification survey, which was scheduled to follow the completion of the current voyage at Quebec. He was a Pakistani national and held an Extra First Class Certificate of Competency as Marine Engineer, issued to him by the Government of Pakistan, after he passed the examination in the United Kingdom. He resided in the USA, near the B+H offices in Stamford, Connecticut.

From 1987 the Superintendent worked for a shipping company as technical manager. He moved to chartering and operations in 1990 and later became general manager of a subsidiary company. He then joined B+H in October 1991 as Assistant Vessel Manager. In November 1992 he became Vessel Manager with responsibility for four ships, including BRAER. On taking over these vessels he started a programme of voyages of about 12 days duration on each vessel. His passage on BRAER was to be his third such voyage.

2.7 Master and Crew

BRAER was manned with a total crew of 29, exclusive of the Superintendent and the four Polish fitters. The crew included the Master, Radio Officer, three deck officers, four engineer officers and an electrical officer. The ratings in the deck department were the Bosun, three able seamen, two ordinary seamen, a deck cadet, a deck fitter and a pumpman. In the engine department were three motormen, an engine fitter, an engine cadet and a wiper. Four catering ratings completed the complement. The Master, Chief Engineer and First Assistant Engineer were Greek nationals and the other officers and all the ratings were Filipino nationals.

The following personnel are referred to in this Report:

- The Master was aged 46 and first went to sea in 1966. All his sea service had been spent in tankers. He was issued with a licence to serve as Captain Class A by The Hellenic Republic in 1980 and was first appointed Master in 1985, since when he had commanded ten crude oil tankers of 35,000 dwt up to 423,000 dwt. He also held a Licence of Competence as Master On Ocean Going Vessels of Any Tonnage, issued by The Republic of Liberia in October 1990. The Master was recruited by B+H upon application to their representative in Piraeus in October 1992 and later that month took command of BRAER in Germany.

7

- The Radio Officer was aged 50 and was issued with a 1st Class Radiotelegraphy Certificate by The Government of the Philippines in 1972. He had served in vessels on world wide trading since 1981 and also held a 1st Class Radiotelegraphy Licence, issued by The Republic of Liberia in 1990. He joined BRAER in June 1992.

- The Chief Officer was aged 36 and was issued with a Certificate of Authorisation to Navigate as a Chief Mate on Merchant Vessels of any Gross Tons on any Sea or Ocean by The Republic of the Philippines in 1986. He first served as Chief Officer in 1988 and subsequently served for 11 months on a crude oil tanker in that capacity. He also held a Licence of Competence as Chief Mate, issued by The Republic of Liberia in February 1990. He joined BRAER in October 1992.

- The Chief Engineer was aged 52 and had served at sea since 1960. He was issued with an A Class (1st Class Engineer) licence by The Hellenic Republic in 1975. Most of his service at sea had been in cargo vessels, but he had served on a number of tankers since 1984, when he was issued with a Licence of Competence as Chief Engineer by The Republic of Liberia. He joined BRAER in November 1992.

- The First Assistant Engineer was aged 47 and had served at sea in various types of vessel since 1971. He was issued with a licence to serve as 2nd Engineer by The Hellenic Republic in 1978 and also held a Licence of Competence as 1st Assistant Engineer, issued by The Republic of Liberia. He joined BRAER on 31 December 1992.

- The Second Assistant Engineer was aged 43 and held a Certificate of Authorisation to serve as Second Marine Engineer, issued by The Republic of the Philippines in 1983 and was to be issued with a Licence of Competence as 2nd Assistant Engineer, by The Republic of Liberia. He joined BRAER in May 1992.

- The Third Assistant Engineer was aged 34 and had served at sea, as a rating and as an officer, since 1980. He held a Certificate of Authorisation to serve as Third Marine Engineer, issued by The Republic of the Philippines in 1991 and also held a Licence of Competence as 3rd Assistant Engineer, issued by The Republic of Liberia. He joined BRAER in October 1992.

3. **NARRATIVE**

Times are UTC *(Universal Co-Ordinated Time)* except where otherwise noted

3.1   BRAER arrived at Mongstad, Norway on 31 December 1992 to load Gullfaks light crude oil for Quebec. On the following day, deballasting was delayed for 18 hours due to the necessary repair to a crack in the feed water pipe to the steam drum of the auxiliary boiler. Loading commenced at 0025 hrs (UTC+1) on 2 January 1993 and was completed at 0837 hrs (UTC+1) on 3 January with the quantity of cargo loaded, according to shore figures provided to the vessel, as 96,515 cubic metres, equivalent to 84,700 tonnes. The vessel's draft was 13.52 metres forward and 14.26 metres aft. Prior to sailing, the Radio Officer obtained a weather forecast and a facsimile synoptic weather chart which he took to the Master and discussed with him: southerly winds of storm force 10 were forecast for sea area Viking. The vessel cleared the loading jetty at 1140 hrs (UTC+1) on 3 January and at 1300 hrs (UTC+1) Full Away Engines was rung and course set to make good 243 ° true in a severe southerly gale. The auxiliary boiler was already on heavy fuel oil and the main engine was changed from diesel oil to heavy fuel oil at 1310 hrs (UTC+1).

3.2   At 1400 hrs (UTC+1), the Bosun reported to the Chief Officer that everything was secured forward and aft. The deck officers were keeping normal sea watches, with the Chief, Second and Third Officers in charge of the 4 to 8, 12 to 4 and 8 to 12 watches, respectively. However, as the Chief Officer had been on cargo duty during the night the other two deck officers shared his afternoon watch on 3 January, the Third Officer relieving the Second Officer at 1800 hrs (UTC+1). The engineer officers were also keeping sea watches, with the First, Second and Third Assistant Engineers keeping the 4 to 8, 12 to 4 and 8 to 12 watches, respectively. Due to the adverse weather conditions, encountered soon after clearing Mongstad, the engine speed was restricted to about 88 rpm. The vessel was rolling and pitching heavily and frequently shipping water on deck. By midnight a speed of about 3 knots had been made since clearing the port. The barometer reading was 1018 mbs, having fallen by 13 mbs in the 12 hours since the vessel left port. At midnight, the clocks were retarded by one hour to UTC.

3.3   During the 0000 hrs to 0400 hrs watch on 4 January, the high and low water level alarms on the auxiliary boiler were sounding, probably due to the rolling of the vessel. To avoid the automatic shutting down, or 'tripping', of the boiler the Second Assistant Engineer adjusted the water level controller to a slightly higher level. Some water was leaking in to the steering flat space through a rope hatch and a ventilator for the deck air compressor; a small portable pump was being used to remove it. On taking over the watch at 0400 hrs, the First Assistant Engineer was told that everything was normal.

3.4   The Chief Officer and his two watch ratings spent the whole of the 0400 hrs to 0800 hrs watch in the wheelhouse. At 0800 hrs a satellite fix of 60°28'N 3°20'E was obtained. This put the vessel about 4 miles to the south of the course line, with an average speed of about 1.5 knots made good since the previous fix at 2300 hrs. The Chief Officer left the bridge shortly after 0800 hrs for his breakfast.

3.5   After breakfast, it was the Chief Officer's usual practice to look around the decks. On this morning, in view of the bad weather, he decided to do some paper work in the cargo control room. On the way there he met the Chief Engineer and it occurred to him that they should both check the security of the four spare pipes which were stowed on the upper deck, against the port side of the engine casing. These pipes were steel, each about five metres in length and up to about half a metre in diameter. They had been secured in a temporary rack by means of spot welding. To avoid going out on deck, the Chief Officer and Chief Engineer went to the crew messroom on the port after side of the boat deck accommodation (one deck above the main deck) and looked down at the pipes through the aft facing window of the messroom. They opened the window to get a better view and saw that some of the pipes were loose and rolling between the engine casing port bulkhead and the ship's side rails as the vessel rolled. They also saw that the loose pipes were banging against the deck air pipes, which were sited just inboard of the side rails. The Chief Engineer also noticed that one of the pipes appeared to be jammed in an athwartship direction. He had previously heard the loose pipes from within the engine control room which was on the deck immediately below the pipes.

3.6   The Chief Officer went to report the loose pipes to the Master, who was alone in his cabin. The Master said that they would have to wait for the weather to subside before anything could be done about them. The Chief Officer left the Master's cabin and went to the crew day room, on the port forward side of the boat deck accommodation, where with the Bosun he watched the port accommodation ladder through one of the forward windows. They were concerned about the ladder, which was located abaft the manifold inboard of the ship's side, as the starboard ladder had been damaged in heavy weather on a previous passage. As the accommodation ladder seemed to be secure, the Chief Officer went to the cargo control room and started his paper work. In the meantime, the Chief Engineer also made a report about the loose pipes to the Master and the Superintendent, who were in the Master's cabin at the time. At 1000 hrs Oseberg Oil Platform was bearing 290° true at a range of 12.2 miles. The vessel was now 4.5 miles south of the course line and had made good 2.2 knots since 0800 hrs. The barometer had ceased to fall and was steady at 1014 mbs. It was still blowing a severe gale from the south.

3.7   The bridge and engine room watches changed again at midday, by which time the course steered had been altered from 190° to 220°, because the vessel was south of the course line. In the engine room, the Second Assistant Engineer again raised the water level control on the boiler, to prevent it from 'tripping out'. At 1400 hrs Oseberg Oil Platform was bearing 010° true at a range of 12.8 miles. This position put the vessel 5.8 miles south of the course line, with a speed of 4 knots made good from the 1000 hrs position. The course steered was altered to 230° gyro to make 251° true, to the North Fair Isle Strait. At about 1500 hrs, the Chief Engineer decided to go to the crew messroom and look at the loose pipes again through the after window. They were still rolling about and he noticed that the air pipes next to the side rails were slightly bent. Before going to the bridge for the 1600 hrs to 2000 hrs watch the Chief Officer also went to the crew messroom to have another look at the loose pipes. He looked again through the after window and saw that the pipes were still rolling across the deck.

3.8   At 1600 hrs the watches changed again. On the bridge, the Second Officer had spent the whole of his afternoon watch inside the wheelhouse. His two watch ratings had been working one hour about on hand steering and lookout duties, the lookout always being kept from inside the wheelhouse. This had been the double watch pattern of bridge duties on all three watches, since the vessel had sailed from Mongstad. The handover of the bridge watch was much the same as for the earlier handovers, the weather conditions not having changed. Nothing in particular was discussed. In the engine room, the Second Assistant Engineer advised the First Assistant Engineer to watch the boiler water level during his forthcoming watch. At 1800 hrs BRAER was passing 3.2 miles to the north of the Odin Gas Platform. She was 2.8 miles to the south of the course line and had made good 5 knots from the 1400 hrs position. The wind strength appeared to be moderating slightly and the engine speed was increased to 100 rpm at 1930 hrs and to 106 rpm at 2000 hrs, by which time the course steered had been altered to 251° gyro. When the bridge watch changed again at 2000 hrs the Chief Officer had spent the whole of his watch in the wheelhouse, as did his two watch ratings. The Master had visited the bridge occasionally during the Chief Officer's watch and during these visits nothing was discussed apart from the weather.

3.9   In the engine room, the 1600 hrs to 2000 hrs watch had passed without incident up to about 1930 hrs, when the auxiliary steam boiler tripped out. It was suspected that this was caused by the rolling of the vessel. The First Assistant Engineer reset the switch and then restarted the boiler. At this time, he noticed that the pressure of steam being delivered by the boiler had dropped to about 7 to 8 Bar. However, by the time the Third Assistant Engineer relieved him at 2000 hrs, the boiler was returning to its usual pressure. On handing over the watch, the First Assistant Engineer told his relief that "everything was OK". On starting his 2000 hrs to 2400 hrs watch, the Third Assistant Engineer carried out his usual rounds and found no difficulties or problems with any of the machinery. The main engine and the auxiliary boiler were running on heavy fuel oil and the starboard generator was running normally on diesel oil.

3.10   At about 2030 hrs the high and low level boiler water alarms started to sound and the steam pressure was around 12 Bar. The water level was fluctuating due to the rolling of the vessel, but the Third Assistant Engineer thought that there was something wrong with the air transmitter which controlled the alarms and decided to shut down the boiler in order to check it. Before shutting down the boiler it was normal procedure to first change the fuel supply to diesel oil fuel, to allow the boiler to be subsequently re-fired. This was done, the boiler being shut down at about 2100 hrs. The Third Assistant Engineer checked the air transmitter, concluded that the adjustment was incorrect and replaced the transmitter with a spare unit. This was completed by about 2130 hrs. The replacement transmitter was then checked and he decided there was another fault, on the low level alarm. The air supply line was drained, after which this alarm appeared to operate normally. The Third Assistant Engineer then started the firing sequence on the boiler, initially at five minute intervals so that the boiler would warm through evenly.

3.11   On the fourth firing sequence, there was a flame failure. The steam pressure had, by this time, fallen to about 3 Bar. The inlet temperature of the main engine fuel had also fallen, from the usual temperature of about 120° centigrade to about 95° centigrade. It was now about 2330 hrs. The Third Assistant Engineer telephoned the Chief Engineer and told him that he intended to change the main engine over to diesel oil. According to his own recollection, he told the Chief Engineer that the main engine fuel temperature was too low and, on being asked why, said that he was having difficulty in firing the boiler; he was not asked why the boiler was not firing. According to the Chief Engineer's recollection, he (the Chief Engineer) was told that the reason for the change was that the steam pressure had dropped; he asked the Third Assistant Engineer why the pressure had dropped and was told that he was changing and adjusting a transmitter. The Chief Engineer agreed to the change of the main engine fuel from heavy oil to diesel oil and later went to bed.

3.12   At 2355 hrs a fix by satellite navigator put the vessel in position 59°49'.6N 0°17'.3E. An average speed of 10 knots had been made good since 1800 hrs. The vessel was still about 2 miles south of the intended course line and, by midnight, the course being steered had been adjusted to 258° gyro. These progressive alterations to starboard in the courses steered since that morning had brought the southerly gale relatively nearer the port beam; although this had made possible the increase in speed, the rolling had also increased and the vessel was continuing to frequently ship water across the main deck. At midnight, the watches changed. It was now 5 January. In a conversation in the engine control room, the Second Assistant Engineer was told by the Third Assistant Engineer that the main engine was running on diesel oil and that the boiler would not fire, although it had been changed to diesel oil prior to its shutdown.

3.13   The two engineers went to check the igniter on the boiler. It was seen that the boiler steam pressure was still about 3 Bar. The igniter was removed, found to be working and replaced. The firing sequence was tried again several times, without success. The coupling in the fuel line to the boiler was then disconnected and the fuel was found to be heavily contaminated with water. The line was drained until uncontaminated fuel was seen to flow from it, then reconnected. The burner was changed and the firing sequence was tried several times without success. The Third Assistant Engineer left the engine room at about 0100 hrs.

3.14   The Superintendent, who had been watching a video film with the Master, left him at about 0200 hrs and decided to visit the engine room before retiring to bed. He noticed that the main engine was running on diesel fuel instead of heavy fuel and found the Second Assistant Engineer, who told him about the problems with the boiler, saying that he was sure the contamination was salt water, because he had tasted it. The fuel line to the boiler was again disconnected, drained of water and sludge and replaced. Further unsuccessful attempts were made to fire the boiler. At about 0230 hrs the Chief Engineer was called and, after his arrival on the boiler flat, further firing attempts were made. The Chief Engineer asked for the fuel line to be disconnected so that he could see the contamination for himself. The line was full of an oil and water mixture. The Chief Engineer, who had now taken charge, tasted a sample of the water himself and found it to be salty. He went to the diesel oil settling tank, opened the drain valve and saw a mixture of water and oil. On opening the diesel oil service tank drain valve, similar contamination was found, but with a less significant proportion of water.

3.15   At 0330 hrs Sumburgh Head was bearing 306° true at a range of 9.4 miles, by radar. A speed of about 10 knots had been made good since midnight. The barometer was again falling. Course was altered to 252° gyro, to make 254° true. This course was to take the vessel through the Fair Isle Channel, passing 7 miles to the south of Sumburgh Head and then south of the IMO (International Maritime Organization) Area to be Avoided (see Figure 1). In the engine room, the Chief Engineer told the watch motorman to start draining the diesel oil settling and service tanks from the drain valves and to continue draining them until uncontaminated diesel oil appeared. At around 0345 hrs the First Assistant Engineer arrived in the engine room for his watch and found the Chief Engineer in the control room and the Superintendent and the Second Assistant Engineer working on the boiler. After taking his own samples from the diesel oil settling and service tanks, he told his watch motorman to continue draining them of contaminated oil.

3.16   The diesel oil in the settling and service tanks was not effectively settling out over the water due to the rolling of the vessel, although the purifier was apparently operating satisfactorily. At around 0400 hrs the engine speed was reduced to approximately 85 rpm to conserve diesel fuel. At about 0410 hrs the Superintendent woke the Master in his cabin and reported the difficulties with the diesel oil. He said that there was water in the diesel tanks and that it was necessary to anchor the vessel in order to drain them fully. The Superintendent accompanied the Master to the bridge and the charts were consulted to find a suitable anchorage. The Chief Officer arrived on the bridge at about the same time, to take over the watch from the Second Officer. In the meantime the Chief Engineer ordered a further reduction of engine speed, to about 45 rpm.

3.17   The Chief Engineer went up to look at the diesel tanks and saw that water was still coming from the drain valves. The contents gauges showed about 9.5 tonnes in the settling tank and about 5 tonnes in the service tank. On the bridge, a suitable anchorage was selected in the Moray Firth, some 100 miles to the south west and at 0436 hrs course was altered to 207° gyro to make 210° true, towards the Moray Firth. The Superintendent left the bridge to return to the engine room. At 0440 hrs, the main engine slowed and then stopped. Two or three minutes later the generator stopped, resulting in a loss of all main power. BRAER was in position 59°41'.5N 1°13'.7W, ten miles almost due south of Sumburgh Head. It was still blowing a severe southerly gale.

3.18   When the generator stopped the 24 volt emergency lighting came on. The Radio Officer woke up, got dressed and went to the radio room. He switched on the emergency power for the radio equipment and waited for instructions. On the bridge the 'not under command' lights were switched on and the vessel's position was entered on the chart and in the log book. In the engine room, unsuccessful attempts were made to start No 1 generator and to re-start No 2 generator. Efforts were then concentrated on draining the water from the diesel oil tanks in the engine room. The Superintendent returned to the bridge, briefed the Master and advised him to place a call to the nearest port to report the situation. The Radio Officer contacted Wick Radio on 2182 Khz at 0500 hrs and passed on the information given to him by the Master. Wick Radio provided a link call connection by landline to Aberdeen Coastguard MRCC (Marine Rescue Co-ordination Centre) and the Radio Officer repeated the information to them.

14

3.19   The message received by Aberdeen Coastguard was as follows:

> "We are a loaded tanker with 34 persons on board broken down
> in position 59°41'N 1°17'W. We have no main engine and no
> emergency power other than battery. I am not in any immediate
> danger. I intend to contact my owner in New York - B+H Ship
> Management (telex and telephone numbers given). After that
> I will come back to you through Wick Radio. This call just to
> alert you to our problem."

The call, timed as 0515 hrs, was acknowledged by Aberdeen Coastguard
who then asked if BRAER needed assistance; the reply was that assistance
was not needed at that moment. BRAER was handed back to Wick Radio,
who left a working channel open for the intended link call to New York.
The Master and the Superintendent left the radio room. BRAER was
drifting towards Sumburgh Head at about two knots, but this was not known
at the time. Aberdeen Coastguard contacted Shetland Coastguard, based
at Lerwick, and relayed the information received from BRAER.

3.20   At 0526 hrs Shetland Coastguard contacted BRAER by VHF and asked the
Master what his intentions were. He replied that he did not require a
helicopter as all the crew were safe, but did require a tug as soon as
possible. The Master also said that his vessel was fully laden with crude oil.
He was asked for his position and rate of drift and replied that BRAER was
about 10 miles south of Sumburgh Head, the rate of drift being "not so
quick". The Master was asked if he wished Shetland Coastguard to contact
Lerwick Port Control and ask them to provide a tug. His answer was in the
affirmative. The Master was then asked if his owners were willing to pay
the commercial rate for towage. His response included the words "I don't
know if you can arrange for the tug because just now I haven't contacted
with my owners in the USA and that's how we will discuss again." Shetland
Coastguard acknowledged this and said that they would pre-warn Lerwick
Port Control of the likelihood that BRAER would require a tug, adding
that it would take two or three hours to reach the vessel and that in the
meantime a helicopter was being alerted in case it was required. The
Master thanked Shetland Coastguard, who responded with the words "Not
at all Sir, if you can come straight back to me when you find out". Shetland
Coastguard having accepted co-ordination of the incident alerted helicopter
R117 at Sumburgh at 0531 hrs.

3.21   At about the time of this initial conversation between the Master (who was
using the VHF set in the wheelhouse) and Shetland Coastguard, the
Superintendent returned to the radio room and made a link call, through
Wick Radio, to the Ship Manager at his home in Stamford USA. The
situation was explained and he was asked to arrange for diesel oil and
compressed air to be sent to the vessel. The Ship Manager acknowledged

this and told the Superintendent to call him back in about ten minutes. The Superintendent returned to the engine room; efforts to start the generators were continuing, but water was still emerging from the drain valves on the diesel oil settling and service tanks and the fuel lines to the generators. At 0534 hrs Shetland Coastguard telephoned Lerwick Port Control and advised them that towage assistance might be required. They discussed the size of BRAER, the capability of the Lerwick tugs, the probability that the larger tugs at Sullom Voe would be needed and the time they would take to reach BRAER.

3.22   The Superintendent made another link telephone call to the Ship Manager, telling him that the situation was worse and that the vessel would need tug assistance, adding that this had already been requested. The Ship Manager said that he was leaving to go to his office. The Superintendent returned once again to the engine room. The lines to the diesel fuel injector pumps were being removed and purged of water and a start was being made to remove the manhole covers on the diesel oil settling and service tanks. More unsuccessful attempts were made to start both generators. With compressed air running low, the hand compressor was brought into use to pump up the emergency air start bottle. At 0537 hrs the Senior Watch Officer (SWO) at Shetland Coastguard telephoned his Duty District Officer (DDO) at his home and briefed him on the situation and on the action he had so far taken. On the matter of towage assistance, the SWO said that the Master of BRAER was contacting his owners in the USA and that he, the SWO, had contacted Lerwick Port Control, who were going to talk to the Lerwick Harbour Master about it. On the matter of BRAER's position and her rate of drift, the DDO was told that the vessel was 10 miles off Sumburgh Head and that the Master had said that she was not drifting very much.

3.23   While the DDO was being briefed, the Master called Shetland Coastguard and asked them to contact his owners in the USA. He provided the telephone number and asked the Coastguard to discuss payment for towage assistance with them. At 0548 hrs Shetland Coastguard called BRAER and asked the Master for his position. The Master responded that the navigational equipment was without power, but his position about 30 minutes previously had been 59°41'N 1°13'W, ten miles south of Sumburgh Head. Coastguard asked the Master if he had been able to speak to his owners. On being told that he had, Coastguard enquired if they had asked for them (Coastguard) to arrange a tow. The Master replied "OK thank you very much arrange tugboat thank you". Coastguard replied "Negative negative a question a question Captain do you require the Coastguards do you want the Coastguard to arrange a tow over". The Master's reply included the words "tell me about the price of tugboat please you er tell me about the price over".

3.24 The conversation continued, from Coastguard - "We do not have any dealings with towage charges the charge is between yourselves and the people who assist you all we can do is arrange for a tug to come to your assistance". The Master then asked if Coastguard had been able to speak to his owners. The reply was negative and the Master asked if Coastguard would do so, using the telephone number he had already given, and discuss towage charges with them. Also at about 0548 hrs, Shetland Coastguard notified Sullom Voe Port Control that tugs might be needed from them. At 0553 hrs, Shetland Coastguard telephoned the number in the USA given them by the Master, and told the person who took the call that they would arrange a tug if he would give them authority to do so. He said he would have to contact the underwriters and would call back. The DDO was telephoned at home and given an update on the situation. The DDO was told that the Master was passing everything to his owners and was not prepared to make a decision, that the owners had been contacted and would revert after speaking to their underwriters and that SETTE MARIE (a fishing vessel) was eight miles south of Hamnivoe Light and could proceed if required. The DDO left his home for Shetland Coastguard.

3.25 At 0556 hrs Lerwick Port Control asked Shetland Coastguard if BRAER had requested a tow. Coastguard said that they did not think so. The conversation included discussion about the likelihood or otherwise of BRAER drifting clear of the land. At 0600 hrs Coastguard alerted a second helicopter, based at RAF Lossiemouth. SETTE MARIE was contacted by Coastguard and asked if she could detect BRAER by radar. She could not, but was asked how long she would take to reach the vessel and requested to stand by on VHF. There followed a conversation between Shetland Coastguard and the fishing vessel TREASURE, who said she had a radar contact of a vessel "dead in the water" six miles south of Sumburgh Head. At about this time, attempts were being made by Sumburgh Air Traffic Control to detect BRAER on their radar. At 0603 hrs Lerwick Port Control telephoned Shetland Coastguard; the capabilities of the Lerwick tugs were again discussed. Lerwick said that there was an anchor handling tug/supply vessel named STAR SIRIUS, in port at Lerwick, which might be made available from her charterers.

3.26 At 0606 hrs Coastguard spoke with the fishing vessel PHILORTH which said that she thought she could detect BRAER on her radar. At 0609 hrs Shetland Coastguard again telephoned B+H in the USA to be told "Yes go ahead we authorise to go and get the tugboat to tow the ship". Coastguard acknowledged this and said they would keep them advised. At 0610 hrs Shetland Coastguard telephoned Sullom Voe Port Control and told them that they required a tug. Port Control queried the terms of the towage and were asked to settle this with the owners in the USA, whose telephone number they would be given if they required it. Rescue Co-ordination Centre in Edinburgh asked RAF Lossiemouth to dispatch a helicopter to Sumburgh. At 0611 hrs Coastguard called BRAER and told her that she

17

was six miles south of Sumburgh Head, that her owners had given them permission to arrange towage and that it would take approximately five hours for tugs to reach her. Coastguard added that they would advise the vessel when a tug was on the way; in the meantime BRAER was asked to try to obtain positions by compass bearings. In the same conversation, BRAER was advised to declare a PAN PAN (Urgency) situation and to consider evacuation of non-essential crew.

3.27   The Master responded "OK its up to you". BRAER was told to stand by on VHF Channel 16. The fishing vessel PHILORTH asked BRAER if she was showing any lights and BRAER replied that she was showing two red lights and PHILORTH acknowledged this, saying that she was quite close. At 0617 hrs helicopter R117 was tasked to proceed to BRAER and commence evacuation. The Master was unwilling to start evacuating crew at that time, but Coastguard advised that the helicopter had already been dispatched and this was accepted by the Master. At 0622 hrs B+H in the USA telephoned Coastguard and asked if a tug had been dispatched. Coastguard replied that a tug had been notified and that a helicopter had been dispatched to evacuate some of the crew. At 0623 hrs Coastguard contacted Lerwick Port Control and enquired whether the Lerwick tug KEBISTER was available to hold BRAER until tugs from Sullom Voe arrived. They were informed that the Lerwick Harbour Master considered that the weather conditions were too bad to consider sending the KEBISTER to sea. Lerwick Port Control then repeated their earlier suggestion that STAR SIRIUS could be made available.

3.28   Coastguard then asked Port Control to contact STAR SIRIUS and ask the vessel to contact them. At 0625 hrs BRAER transmitted an XXX Urgency message on 500 Khz. This message included a position, the fact that the vessel was without main power and that radio communications were by emergency power. Also at 0625 hrs Shetland Coastguard broadcast a PAN PAN Urgency message on VHF Channel 16 to all ships. At 0629 hrs, PHILORTH reported that she was close to BRAER and that Sumburgh Head was bearing 017° 5.2 miles from her. Helicopter R117 was reported as airborne. At 0630 hrs Shetland Towage at Sullom Voe advised that their tug SWAABIE was being prepared for sending to sea as soon as possible and that it would take her at least four to five hours to reach BRAER which Coastguard acknowledged. At 0632 hrs BRAER asked Coastguard to arrange for the helicopter evacuation of 20 persons. At 0634 hrs Lerwick Port Control advised Coastguard that STAR SIRIUS was being prepared to go to the assistance of BRAER.

3.29   The Lerwick Lifeboat was tasked at 0635 hrs. At 0640 hrs, the DDO at Shetland Coastguard telephoned the Director of Marine Emergency Operations (DMEO) at his home in London and briefed him on the essential details of the casualty. He said BRAER was 170° 6.5 miles from Sumburgh Head, with a wind of about 60 knots from a direction 190°. There were two fishing vessels in the area which were providing Coastguard with information on the vessel's position. He said BRAER had been originally reported as being ten miles south of Sumburgh Head at 0519 hrs; tidal information was being consulted to try to estimate the rate of drift. The DMEO was also told that the owners in the USA had been contacted and they had given their agreement for towage to be arranged; a large tug at Sullom Voe had been contacted and was proceeding, it would take five hours to reach the scene; the DMEO was further told that it was hoped to use the services of a supply vessel at Lerwick.

3.30   Helicopter R117 had arrived on scene at 0640 hrs and found BRAER rolling heavily in very heavy seas and winds gusting in excess of 65 knots. Evacuation of crew from the usual helicopter landing area on the foredeck was not possible because that deck was frequently awash, therefore R117 arranged with the Master for evacuation to take place near the stern on the starboard side. At 0641 hrs helicopter R137 was airborne and proceeding from Lossiemouth towards Sumburgh and at 0647 hrs Lerwick Lifeboat proceeded to sea. The District Controller (DC) of Shetland Coastguard was telephoned at his home and briefed on the situation at 0649 hrs; he left his home for Shetland Coastguard. The evacuation of non-essential crew from BRAER by helicopter R117 started at 0654 hrs; the vessel was now about four miles south of Sumburgh Head.

3.31   The Superintendent and the engineers on board BRAER were continuing their efforts to restore power. STAR SIRIUS left Lerwick at 0705 hrs. The DDO gave a further briefing to the DMEO at 0708 hrs; he advised him that STAR SIRIUS was expected to be on scene in two to two and a half hours time and that if BRAER continued to drift in the direction of the wind she would probably ground, although this was not certain and she could drift clear of the land. The owners asked Coastguard for an update of the situation at 0710 hrs; following the update, the owners were told that it would not be practicable to provide compressed air and diesel oil to BRAER at that time. At 0722 hrs helicopter R137, which was on its way to the scene, reported that they had the casualty on radar and it was approximately four miles from Sumburgh Head. STAR SIRIUS advised Coastguard that she had cleared Lerwick Harbour at 0736 hrs and expected to be on scene in two and a half hours. Helicopter R137 arrived on scene at 0740 hrs, stood off for instructions and at 0742 hrs advised Coastguard that the land was two and a half miles away. R137 said that they had sufficient fuel for another hour and a half on scene and also advised that at BRAER's rate of drift, she would be aground within that time.

3.32   By 0807 hrs the evacuation of 16 crew from BRAER had been completed and helicopter R117 left the scene for Sumburgh Airport. Coastguard asked the Master what his intentions were. There followed discussion between the Master and Shetland Coastguard as to whether or not the vessel was to be finally abandoned. At 0813 hrs helicopter R137 advised the Master to abandon as the pilot considered that there was little time left to evacuate the remaining 18 crew before the vessel grounded; at that time it appeared that the vessel would continue to drift in a northerly direction into West Voe, close west of Sumburgh Head. The Superintendent made a link call to his Ship Manager in the USA. He told him that the vessel was very near the rocks and that they were being advised to abandon ship. At 0815 hrs the tug SWAABIE left Sullom Voe; the tug TIRRICK followed fifteen minutes later. At 0825 hrs helicopter R137 commenced winching up the remaining crew. BRAER was just half a mile south east of Horse Island and it still appeared that she would drift into West Voe.

3.33   At 0827 hrs the Master decided to abandon the vessel. At 0840 hrs helicopter R137 reported that BRAER was bearing 240° at a range of one mile from Sumburgh Head. Helicopter R117 was back on scene. At 0845 hrs the DC gave an updated briefing to the DMEO; he gave the position of BRAER and said that it looked as if she would not drift clear of the point; the DMEO was also informed that the evacuation of the remaining crew was proceeding without any problems. The DMEO left his home for the Marine Emergency Incident Room (MEIR) at Marine Directorate Headquarters in London. The evacuation was completed at 0854 hrs and helicopter R137 proceeded to Sumburgh Airport, reporting the position of BRAER as being 260° 0.75 miles from Sumburgh Head. The Lerwick Lifeboat was stood down. Helicopter R117 reported the position of BRAER as being 59°49'.4N 1°18'.3W* and said that they were remaining on scene to watch the vessel's drift. At 0857 hrs the Coastguard Sector Officer, who was observing BRAER from the shore, estimated that the vessel was three quarters of a mile from Sumburgh Head and looking as if she would ground in West Voe.

3.34   Helicopter R137 landed at Sumburgh at 0900 hrs. At 0905 hrs helicopter R117 reported that BRAER appeared to be drifting towards the north-west, although the predicted set of the tidal stream had not yet turned in that direction. At 0909 hrs the Shetland Islands Council helicopter reported the position of BRAER as one and a half miles south-east of Horse Island*. The DC contacted the Regional Controller (RC) at 0914 hrs and obtained his agreement to make arrangements to put the Master and some members of the crew back on board to let go the anchors. At 0917 hrs helicopter R117 reported BRAER as bearing 199° magnetic distance 3.2 miles from

*   These positions are in conflict with the general run of other reported positions of BRAER.

20

Sumburgh Airport Radio Beacon. At 0926 hrs the DC contacted the Master who was at Sumburgh Airport and asked whether the anchors could be let go if it were possible to land him and somebody else on board the vessel. After considerable discussion, with some language difficulties, the Master agreed that the anchors could be let go, but only if the vessel drifted into water of less than 30 metres depth. At 0934 hrs helicopter R117 discussed with Coastguard the possibility of landing one or two people on the bow of BRAER.

3.35   The DMEO was given a briefing at 0935 hrs; he was told that BRAER "seemed to be getting around in a very small tight circle" and it was hoped to land somebody on the bow by helicopter to drop the anchors and that this was under discussion (see Figure 2).

Later in this briefing, the DMEO was told that STAR SIRIUS was half a mile from the casualty, which was in position 215° 1.4 miles from Sumburgh Head. Shetland Coastguard were given a weather forecast at 0937 hrs; this predicted severe gale force 9 for the next 18 hours, veering south-west and increasing to storm force 10 gusting to force 12. The fishing vessel PHILORTH, which was close to BRAER, reported that the vessel was three quarters of a mile from Horse Island and appeared to be closing with it. PHILORTH was asked to remain with BRAER, since there was a possibility that there would be attempts to drop the anchors and it would be useful to have a fishing vessel nearby in case someone fell overboard.

3.36   At 0939 hrs Shetland Coastguard were notified that two marine pilots were on their way by road from Sullom Voe to Sumburgh and would be given a police escort from Lerwick. At 0944 hrs the tug SWAABIE called Shetland Coastguard and advised that she and the tug TIRRICK, hoped to be on scene in four and a half hours. The DC gave a briefing to MEIR at 0945 hrs and said that Coastguard were contemplating putting the Master back on board BRAER if weather conditions permitted. At this time STAR SIRIUS asked Coastguard if it was the intention to put a man on the tanker to drop the anchors; the answer was in the affirmative, but only if the vessel was in water of less than 30 metres depth. After acknowledging this, STAR SIRIUS said that she was in a position where she could get a line to the tanker with a rocket line, but could not do so until there was some assistance on the vessel.

3.37   The Master of STAR SIRIUS reported that the deck around the accommodation at the after end of BRAER was "fairly dry". Coastguard asked for the conditions at the bow; STAR SIRIUS replied that there was spray on the raised forecastle head, but no "green water" there. STAR SIRIUS advised Coastguard that the depth of water under BRAER at that time was approximately 50 metres. STAR SIRIUS confirmed that it would be better to use the stern rather than the bow in an attempt to connect a tow. Her Master went on to describe to Coastguard how he proposed a tow could be set up, if men could be landed on BRAER's stern by helicopter. BRAER was at this time 8 cables south-south-west of Horse Island and drifting slowly past it. Helicopter R117 then entered the VHF conversation (at 0951 hrs) and suggested to Coastguard that they should verify with Sumburgh Airport that there were two seamen available from BRAER's crew.

3.38   At 0954 hrs BRAER was 240° 6 cables from the south-western tip of Horse Island and by 1005 hrs was 250° 6.5 cables from Horse Island. The DC spoke to the Master at 1010 hrs; he explained, with some difficulty, that a tug was standing by BRAER and needed some members of the crew to take a light line and make it fast to one of the heavier lines, which would then be heaved on board the tug. The Master agreed that five of his crew members and the two marine pilots would be landed on the vessel. The DC told the Master that Coastguard would get in touch with him later. STAR SIRIUS gave an updated position of BRAER at 1014 hrs, which was 280° 7 cables from Horse Island. Helicopter R117 returned to Sumburgh to refuel. STAR SIRIUS asked Coastguard if there was any likelihood of the helicopter bringing crew members back to the scene. At 1016 hrs Coastguard confirmed with the helicopter base that R117 would be used to land five crew and the two marine pilots on BRAER. Attempts were being made to locate BRAER's crew at the airport. In a discussion with the Pilot of R117, the DC confirmed the arrangement and said that the police should be bringing the crew to the heliport.

3.39   By 1026 hrs BRAER was bearing 209° 6.8 cables from Lady's Holm and drifting past it. At 1051 hrs helicopter R117 reported that they had four crew members from the vessel and the two marine pilots from Sullom Voe and were just starting up engines. BRAER had passed Lady's Holm and was now drifting towards Garths Ness, on the west side of the Bay of Quendale. At 1052 hrs STAR SIRIUS estimated to Shetland Coastguard that BRAER would ground on Garths Ness in 30 minutes. Helicopter R117 left Sumburgh at 1055 hrs for BRAER, which was at this time 190° 6.5 cables from Garths Ness and drifting towards it at a speed of 1.7 knots. On board R117 were the Master, the Chief Officer, the Bosun and the Superintendent, together with the Port Safety Manager of Shetland Islands Coun|cil and one of the Marine Pilots who had travelled from Sullom Voe.

3.40   When the helicopter was over the starboard quarter of BRAER the Winchman was landed on the deck first, followed by the Port Safety Manager and the Superintendent. Helicopter R117 then stood off while STAR SIRIUS fired a rocket line, which missed the stern. R117 then lowered the Chief Officer and stood off again while a second rocket line was fired. This landed on the port side of the boat deck and became entangled in the port lifeboat davits. The Port Safety Manager had gone straight to the bridge after being landed; he used the vessel's VHF radio to contact STAR SIRIUS who confirmed the plan to send a rope messenger across to the vessel. The Port Safety Manager then went down to the poop to find the Winchman trying to clear the entangled rocket line. The Port Safety Manager cut it free with his knife. The Superintendent was trying to clear the end of one of the ship's mooring ropes from its drum on the mooring winch, assisted by the Chief Officer. The Winchman and the Port Safety Manager passed the rocket line aft, put it through a fairlead and then heaved on it, assisted by the Superintendent.

3.41   The rope messenger had been made fast to the rocket line and was being paid out from STAR SIRIUS. The intention was to secure the messenger rope to one of the mooring ropes on BRAER and then heave the mooring rope across to STAR SIRIUS, using her winch power. When the end of the messenger was about half way to the stern of BRAER the action of the sea pulled the rocket line out of the hands of the three men. About a minute later, a large wave lifted the stern of BRAER and the vessel landed heavily on rocks on the west side of Garths Ness. The helicopter returned and all four men were safely recovered and returned to Sumburgh. The time of the grounding was recorded as 1119 hrs.

4. SEQUENCE AND TIMETABLE OF EVENTS

The Narrative in the preceding section is very detailed because it is important to give all the facts as recorded by those who were involved in the incident. It is appreciated that it may not be easy to pick out the main events from that section therefore the following is a timetable of those events:

Time	Event
3 January	
1300 hrs (UTC+1)	BRAER sails from Mongstad.
4 January	
1000 hrs (approx)	Spare pipes on BRAER noted to have broken free from the securing arrangements.
2100 hrs	Auxiliary boiler shut down.
2330 hrs	Difficulties in refiring auxiliary boiler. Main engine changed over to diesel oil.
5 January	
0030 hrs	Salt water contamination of diesel oil supply to auxiliary boiler discovered.
0200 hrs	Superintendent goes to engine room.
0230 hrs	Chief Engineer called to engine room.
0230 hrs - 0330 hrs	Water contamination of diesel oil settling and service tanks discovered. Attempts to drain off the water.
0400 hrs	Engine speed reduced to conserve diesel fuel.
0410 hrs	Master advised of situation and decision made to proceed to an anchorage in the Moray Firth. Water still being drained off from the diesel oil settling and service tanks.
0440 hrs	Main engine stops. BRAER approximately 10 miles south of Sumburgh Head.
0442 hrs	Generator stops, all main power lost. Attempts to drain off water from diesel oil continues.

0515 hrs	Master advises Coastguard that his vessel is broken down but he does not require assistance.
0526 hrs	Coastguard contacts BRAER to ask his intentions. The Master responds he does not require a helicopter but does require a tug as soon as possible. Superintendent phones his superior in the USA advising him of the situation.
0531 hrs	Coastguard alert helicopter R117.
0534 hrs	Coastguard advise Lerwick Port Control that tug assistance might be required.
0536 hrs	Superintendent phones his superior in the USA a second time and advises him that tug assistance would be needed. Attempts to drain off water from diesel oil continues.
0600 hrs	BRAER reported to be 6 miles south of Sumburgh Head.
0609 hrs	BRAER's owners in the USA authorise Coastguard to arrange a tug.
0611 hrs	Coastguard advise BRAER that towage has been authorised by her owners.
0617 hrs	R117 tasked to proceed to BRAER.
0634 hrs	STAR SIRIUS being prepared to go to assistance of BRAER.
0640 hrs	R117 on scene at BRAER.
0641 hrs	R137 airborne from Lossiemouth.
0654 hrs	Evacuation of non-essential persons from BRAER by R117 commences. BRAER approximately 4 miles south of Sumburgh Head.
0705 hrs	STAR SIRIUS leaves Lerwick.
0740 hrs	R137 on scene at BRAER.
0807 hrs	Evacuation of non-essential persons complete.
0825 hrs	Evacuation of remaining crew from BRAER by R137 commences.
0854 hrs	Evacuation of remaining crew complete. BRAER approximately 0.75 miles west from Sumburgh Head.

0914 hrs	Decision taken to try to put people back on the bow of BRAER to let go the anchors. (This idea was abandoned for helicopter safety reasons).
0935 hrs	STAR SIRIUS half a mile from BRAER.
0945 hrs	STAR SIRIUS in position to fire a rocket line to BRAER.
1010 hrs	Decision taken to put people back on the stern of BRAER to try and take a line from STAR SIRIUS. Difficulties being experienced in locating the necessary crew members.
1055 hrs	R117 leaves Sumburgh with six people to land on BRAER. Four persons land on stern of BRAER. Rocket line from STAR SIRIUS successfully passed to BRAER but when the attached messenger line is mid way between the two vessels the action of the sea pulls the line from their hands.
1119 hrs	Before another attempt to take a line can be made the vessel grounds and those on board are winched off.

PART II   CONSIDERATION OF POSSIBLE FACTORS

5.   TECHNICAL MAINTENANCE

5.1   In common with the majority of vessels currently at sea, a system of 'Planned Maintenance' of both machinery and hull was practised on BRAER.   The Inspectors were advised that the system was based on a combination of mandatory and classification society survey requirements, manufacturers' recommendations and the operational experience of the ship's staff.   The Chief Engineer was responsible for all machinery maintenance and repairs and the Chief Officer was responsible for the operational maintenance of deck machinery and fittings, including air pipes. The Deck Fitter was normally assigned to carry out such deck maintenance work as was required, under the direction of the Chief Officer.

5.2   Overhauls and inspections of the larger items of machinery, which were operated on a running hours basis, were carried out after a pre-determined number of hours under the maintenance system.   Pumps and other smaller items were inspected and overhauled on a discretionary basis.   The system on board did not include daily or weekly maintenance items.   The items covered under the time based system included the main engine, diesel alternators, steam generator and fresh water generator.   For the smaller auxiliaries such as pumps, valves and domestic machinery, repairs and maintenance were carried out on a priority basis as decided by the Chief Engineer.

5.3   Monthly returns relating to machinery items on a running hours basis were made and at the end of each month, deck and engine maintenance reports were submitted to Head Office, together with details of spares used and received.   The Superintendent, during his vessel familiarisation voyage, was to examine the current planned maintenance system with a view to converting it to a fully computerised system, similar to those he had installed on other vessels under his control.

5.4   Maintenance work carried out on the two preceding voyages included inspection of the economiser internals and the changing of the fuel injectors and scavenge valves for Nos 1 and 2 main engine units; this work was done in mid-November 1992, prior to departure from New York for Mongstad. During the passage various minor maintenance repairs were carried out including work to the ballast pump, general service pump and starboard boiler feed pump.   The port side inert gas fan impeller was found to be out of balance and arrangements were made for it to be removed and repaired on the vessel's return to New York.   During the stay in Mongstad, the scavenge valves for Nos 3 and 4 main engine units were cleaned and

27

changed. On the return passage to New York, various other maintenance work was carried out. A work list, together with a request for a 'riding crew' of maintenance fitters for the next voyage, was submitted to Head Office. On arrival in New York (in December 1992) the fuel injectors on Nos 3 and 4 main engine units were changed and the balancing of the port inert gas fan impeller was put in hand.

5.5   On the ballast voyage from New York to Mongstad no major repairs were undertaken, but minor repairs were carried out as required. During this passage, the auxiliary boiler and the economiser adequately supplied the steam demand despite a leak developing on the boiler feed pump line three days prior to arrival at Mongstad. After berthing, the boiler was shut down to allow a welding repair to the boiler feed line to be carried out.

5.6   As agreed by Head Office, four Polish fitters joined the vessel at Mongstad to undertake various maintenance and repair work during the forthcoming voyage to Quebec. This work was to be in two parts: work to be carried out in port prior to departure from Mongstad and work to be carried out at sea during the passage.

5.7   By the evening of 4 January, all the 'in port' items had been completed and the fitters were engaged in 'at sea' items. Whilst in Mongstad, the engine room crew had also changed the fuel injectors on main engine unit Nos 5, 6 and 7 as well as the fuel pump plunger and guides on No 4 main engine unit. After BRAER sailed the day work crew were engaged in various cleaning and equipment securing duties whilst the two ship's fitters and the Electrical Officer carried out various maintenance work in the engine room.

5.8   Projected maintenance work was discussed between the Chief Engineer and the Superintendent during the afternoon of 4 January, when the Chief Engineer described the work which he considered should be carried out at the next repair period. This 'off hire' period was scheduled to be after discharge of the present cargo in Quebec, a period of five days being suggested. The work was intended to be undertaken jointly by the ship's crew, the Polish 'riding crew' and the repair yard.

       The list of overhaul work was based on a combination of running hours and a general lowering of efficiency of the machinery.

5.9   Subsequent to this meeting, the Superintendent faxed a progress report and a list of items requiring attention to his Head Office, in Stamford USA.

Some of the work mentioned in the report would have been undertaken during the voyage, but other repair items were dependent on the availability of spare material on board. The items listed by the Superintendent, had they been known at Mongstad, would not necessarily have prevented the vessel from sailing. They would form the basis for the preparation of a repair specification covering the next repair and dry dock period.

5.10   The Inspectors were not able to get on board and inspect the vessel but the condition of the machinery, according to the available evidence, suggests that although a backlog of repair and maintenance work had built up, this was being rectified. The Chief Engineer's request for a 'riding crew' of four fitters to assist in repairs is common practice these days and in the opinion of the Inspectors there had been no evidence of neglect or lack of maintenance.

6.   SEAWORTHINESS

6.1   The seaworthiness of vessels such as BRAER depends to a large extent on standards of compliance with the Conventions, flag state and classification society requirements. These standards are usually monitored and enforced as necessary through surveys and inspections by flag states and the classification societies. In addition, unannounced inspections may be carried out by certain port states and flag states. Owners and charterers may also carry out their own inspections when they see this as necessary.

6.2   Records of inspections of BRAER in 1992 show that she was inspected four times under port state control procedures in Europe, Canada and the United States; only one report showed a deficiency, which was minor. Furthermore, a flag state annual inspection was carried out in June of that year at Sullom Voe by an appointed surveyor on behalf of the Liberian Marine Inspection Division; in the following month the vessel was inspected in Canada by Ultramar, her charterers. Neither report showed any significant deficiencies relevant to the seaworthiness of the vessel.

6.3   The statutory convention certificates relating to seaworthiness are the Cargo Ship Safety Construction Certificate and the International Load Line Certificate. Both these certificates were issued to BRAER by Det Norske Veritas, the classification society. They were valid to July 1994, subject to satisfactory intermediate and annual surveys and inspections. The last Intermediate Safety Construction Survey and the last Annual Load Line Inspection were both carried out in May 1992; the items subject to survey and inspection included main and auxiliary machinery and boilers and weather deck air pipes to tanks. The engine room stores hatch and some ventilators required gaskets. These minor deficiencies were recorded as rectified in the following month.

6.4   The term 'seaworthiness' could be interpreted to mean the vessel's fitness to complete safely the contemplated voyage through the worst weather likely to be encountered. BRAER was a vessel engaged in world wide trading, latterly on North Atlantic crossings between Europe and North America at all times of the year. Tankers, by virtue of their relatively high degree of sub-division and stability, the small size of their cargo hatches and the nature of the cargo they carry, are permitted to load to a smaller freeboard than other vessels. Consequently, in heavy weather conditions it is not unusual for a loaded tanker to ship large quantities of water on deck. Openings on the weather deck need to be properly protected from damage and loss of weathertightness and movable objects, not part of the vessel's superstructure, need to be efficiently secured against movement.

6.5   The four spare steel pipes which BRAER was carrying on deck were described in some detail by the Chief Officer: two of about 250mm in diameter, two larger ones of about 450mm in diameter and all about five metres in length. Two of them are visible in aerial photographs taken after the grounding (see Figure 3). It is not clear when these pipes were first put on board or for what purpose, but they were certainly there in October 1992; since then BRAER had made three loaded passages, two of them across the North Atlantic in the winter season. The most likely use for the pipes would have been for cargo, ballast or inert gas pipeline renewals on deck, and it is estimated that the weights would have been approximately 80 kg for each of the smaller pipes and approximately 1,000 kg for each of the larger ones.

6.6   The pipes were stacked in a fore and aft direction against the port side of the engine casing, on two timber bearers of 100mm by 50mm cross section (see Figure 4). The two larger pipes lay side by side on the bearers, with the smaller pipes on top. They were held against the casing by two metal uprights, one near each end of the stack and welded to the deck. They may also have been lashed together by rope or wire. This is how the pipes were secured at the time the Chief Officer first saw them after he joined the vessel in October 1992.

6.7   In his evidence, the Chief Officer said that at that time he considered that the pipes were secured well enough for summer conditions, but further securing was needed for winter season passages. In early November, he made his concerns known to the Master who agreed with him and suggested the matter should be discussed with the Engineers, whom he considered were responsible for the pipes. The Chief Officer duly spoke with the Chief and First Assistant Engineers. The Chief Engineer has stated that in that discussion he had suggested that the pipes should be stowed elsewhere on the vessel, because he considered there was a chance of them breaking loose in heavy weather.

6.8   The outcome of the discussion was that the pipes would remain where they were, but they would be additionally secured to hold them to the deck and against the casing. In November 1992, during the ballast passage between New York and Mongstad, the Deck Fitter assisted by engine ratings built a rack around the pipes. The existing uprights were replaced by three longer angle bars extending above the top of the stack. Three similar uprights were inserted between the pipes and the casing. Flat bars were then laid across the stack and bolted to the uprights. The uprights were welded to the deck and where these and the flat bars bore against the pipes they were spot welded. The Chief Officer has also stated that some of the pipes were spot welded together and additional short bars were placed between adjacent pipes and also spot welded. He inspected the rack when it was completed and was satisfied that the pipes had been made as secure

31

as possible. The finished rack was also inspected by the Master at Mongstad. On the following loaded passage back to New York in early December, heavy weather was encountered and the pipes remained secure.

6.9   Although the details of the way the pipes were additionally secured have not been corroborated by other officers, the Inspectors have no reason to doubt the supporting evidence of the Master and Chief Engineer that the pipes had been additionally secured with welding in November 1992. However, it should have been clear that the pipes were in an exposed position and the welding was not enough to prevent the stack from breaking loose in the very heavy weather conditions experienced on BRAER's last voyage.

6.10   Other items of equipment were kept on deck. About twenty oxygen and acetylene bottles were on the weather deck in the midships space between the accommodation house and the engine casing. Most of these were in brackets fitted along the after side of the accommodation, others were in a free standing cage which was secured against movement. On the starboard side of the boat deck, aft of the lifeboat, were about six 200 litre drums of hydraulic oil. These were lashed by rope. The aerial photographs taken after the grounding are not detailed enough to show these other items of equipment. They were stowed in less vulnerable positions and there is no evidence to suggest that they too had broken loose.

6.11   It is of course certain that the four pipes had been broken loose by the action of the heavy rolling and the seas shipped over the port side, during the passage from Mongstad. From the evidence, the pipes were first seen to be loose and rolling about the deck during the morning of 4 January. The vessel had already been at sea, in much the same weather conditions, for some 21 hours.

6.12   The Master was allowing considerable leeway during the earlier part of the passage, in fact at midnight on 3 January the vessel was steering almost south to make good a course of 243° an allowance of some 50°. On this heading, the wind and seas were on the port bow and the pipes would have been protected to some extent by the bulk of the accommodation superstructure forward of their stowage; furthermore, the rolling would not have been so heavy on this heading. The leeway allowance later proved to be excessive and 30° of it was removed, probably shortly after the 1000 hrs fix on 4 January. (The word 'probably' has been used because the times of these course changes and allowances for leeway had not been recorded in the deck log book). From 1000 hrs the weather was much nearer the beam and the pipes would have become totally exposed to the direct action of the seas shipped across the port side of the deck. The rolling would also have increased. It therefore seems likely that the pipes had only recently broken loose when the Chief Officer and Chief Engineer first saw them rolling about from the crew messroom window.

6.13   The Chief Officer and Chief Engineer saw that the pipes were landing heavily against the deck air pipes on the port side and both officers reported the loose pipes to the Master. It was then decided that no action could be taken for as long as the weather conditions persisted. The same officers each said that they made individual return visits to the messroom in the afternoon to have another look at the pipes. This suggests that they did perhaps have doubts about the decision to do nothing about them. However, no further reports appear to have been made to the Master and nobody seems to have taken any further interest in the loose pipes after 1600 hrs on 4 January.

6.14   The port double bottom diesel oil storage tank was provided with two deck air pipes, one for each end of the tank. The stem of each air pipe extended 600mm above the deck and fitted to it was a float seal type head of 160mm in height (see Figure 5). The head was designed to allow air and overflow oil to escape from the tank and prevent water from entering it. These and other air pipes to fuel oil tanks were provided with 'savealls' around the base. The purpose of savealls is to prevent small overflows of oil from escaping overside and causing pollution. Although they would give some structural protection to the bases of the air pipes, their limited strength and height above the deck would have provided little if any resistance to damage from the much larger and heavier loose pipes. The forward air pipe was in way of frame 38 and opposite the after part of the accommodation block; the outside diameter of the stem was 120mm. The after air pipe, with a smaller outside stem diameter of 80mm, was in way of frame 29 and directly opposite the engine casing, where the spare pipes had been stowed. (See Figure 4 indicating the location of various air pipes)

6.15   Five further air pipes were located opposite the spare pipe stowage on the port side of the engine casing. These served void and other spaces and small non-fuel tanks. All these air pipes, which can be seen in the photographs taken aboard two identical sister ships, were susceptible to damage from the loose and rolling pipes in the very heavy weather conditions prevailing at the time. The loose pipes were seen to be landing heavily against the air pipes on the morning of 4 January and in the afternoon the Chief Engineer saw that some of the air pipes had been bent. It is not known whether or not the after air pipe to the port double bottom diesel oil tank was among those damaged at that time, because that air pipe was outside the field of view from the messroom window. However, it is highly likely that it was and it is almost certain that this air pipe was substantially damaged some time prior to the start of the problems with the boiler.

6.16   When the four volunteers boarded BRAER after the abandonment, it was found that a large portion of the ship's side rail was missing from the port side, extending from near frame 31 to near frame 24. The port double bottom diesel oil tank aft air pipe was at frame 29. There was a further piece of rail missing approximately in way of frames 17/19. The gaps in the rail can be clearly seen in the photographs (see Figure 6) and one of the volunteers recalled noticing that the broken ends of rail had been forced outwards. It can also be seen that the two visible loose pipes were lying in almost athwartship positions, one on each side of the deck. The one on the port side, which appears to be one of the 450mm pipes, can be seen up against the fore side of one of the mooring bitts; the outboard end of it appears to be jammed in the side rail. The other pipe, probably one of the 250mm ones, is seen in a similar position, but on the after side of the bitts, with its outboard end similarly jammed in the starboard side rail. The Chief Officer and Chief Engineer could not have failed to notice the missing sections of side rail, if this particular damage had happened before their final observations through the messroom window on the afternoon of 4 January. It must therefore be assumed that it happened sometime during that evening, or even later.

6.17   A large loaded tanker invariably has a large metacentric height, giving a short period of roll. From the morning of 4 January, with the seas nearly abeam, BRAER would have been rolling 'stiffly', with considerable dynamic forces being exerted on her weather deck around the extremity of each roll. A heavy loose object on the deck would have had the potential to acquire considerable kinetic energy which, towards the extremity of the roll, could have effectively projected it to the ship's side with the force of a battering ram. The relatively weak air pipes would not, and the ship's side rails certainly did not, withstand such forces.

6.18   It is therefore almost certain that the port double bottom diesel oil tank aft air pipe was damaged by the loose pipes, enough to allow sea water to enter it and breach BRAER's watertight integrity and seaworthiness. There is a possibility that the forward port air pipe was breached as well, but this is less likely because that air pipe was in a less exposed position, partially protected by the pillar support to the boat deck above. However, it must be considered a strong possibility that one or both of the air pipes to the starboard double bottom diesel oil tank and the air pipe to the diesel oil settling and service tanks were damaged, since at least one of the loose pipes had found its way to the starboard side of the deck.

7. MANNING

7.1 The Greek Master, Chief Engineer and First Assistant Engineer had been recruited by B+H through their agent in Piraeus, Greece. The Filipino officers and all the ratings were recruited by Singa Ship Management AS of Oslo through their Filipino subsidiary, Micronesia Manpower Resources Corporation of Manila. The manning of large tankers with non-national crews is now a common practice, particularly on vessels on the Liberian and other open registers. On such vessels the absence of specific nationality requirements allows owners to employ officers and ratings from countries which are party to the International Convention on Standards of Training, Certification and Watchkeeping 1978 (STCW). Greece and the Philippines are both party states to STCW.

7.2 The previous First Assistant Engineer, a Filipino, had left the vessel at short notice during December 1992 in New York; it appears that there had been personal differences between him and the Chief Engineer, who said that the First Assistant Engineer had wanted to leave because there was too much work to do. Since his Greek replacement did not join until the vessel reached Mongstad, BRAER had made the passage from New York with deficient engine room manning. It is not, however, likely that this was a contributory factor to the accident.

7.3 The Master and the two Greek engineers held valid Greek certificates for a vessel of BRAER's class and trade. STCW requires that Convention certificate holders should have their continued proficiency proved after five years. For the Greek Master and Engineers, this would have become due in 1989, five years after the Convention came into force. Holders of United Kingdom certificates have their continued proficiency recorded by an endorsement on the certificate. However, the Inspectors were advised by the Greek Ministry of Mercantile Marine that they do not require re-validation in the form of an endorsement or a special document. The Greek certificate holders also held Liberian licences, which were issued on production of their Greek certificates. The Liberian authorities have an examination system of their own but they also accept the certificates of other countries whose standards are acceptable to them. Liberian licences are not re-validated either, a new licence is issued instead. The Filipino officers all held appropriate Filipino certificates. As in the case of the Greek certificate holders, they had also been issued with Liberian licences. The ratings all held the appropriate qualifications which had been issued by the Philippine authorities.

35

7.4   The manning on BRAER, a total of 29 crew excluding the Superintendent and four Polish fitters, was perhaps in excess of the complement one would currently expect to find on other and similar vessels. However, it is considered that the quality of the senior manning on BRAER, while no doubt typical of many hundreds of other vessels trading at sea today, left much to be desired. The actions of individual senior officers are commented upon in later sections of this Report.

7.5   It is sometimes claimed that multi-national crews on board vessels can lead to language problems. This can manifest itself in two ways: communication problems between those on board and communication problems between ship and shore. There were four nationalities represented on BRAER at the time of the incident: Greek, Filipino, Pakistani and Polish.

In an investigation such as this one it is difficult to judge whether the different languages of the various nationalities did create problems on board. However during the interviews carried out with the various crew members during the course of the investigation the Inspectors came to the conclusion that there were no major problems between the senior engineers who were Greek and the other engineers who were Filipino. The same applies to communications between the Superintendent and the officers on board.

There were misunderstandings between the Master and the Coastguard due to language difficulties and these are addressed in Section 14 of this Report. English is the accepted international language of the marine world and although the Master seemed reasonably proficient in it, it is understandable that he would have been under some stress at the time of the incident, both whilst still on board and after he had been brought ashore. It is therefore not surprising that he had difficulty in comprehending the true meaning of some of the questions which were put to him in a language which was not his mother tongue.

Claims were made that there were problems with the communication between the vessel and their office in the USA but it is more likely this was due to poor reception conditions rather than language difficulties.

8.   ROUTE TAKEN

8.1   The voyage clause in the charter party did not specify the route to be taken by BRAER for her passage to Quebec, neither did it specify the time to be taken.   However in all charter party agreements there is an implied stipulation that the vessel must proceed on the voyage with reasonable dispatch and without unjustifiable deviation from the usual route, except for certain specified and justifiable reasons as set out in the deviation clause. There were only two alternative routes avoiding the Orkney and Shetland Islands: north about (north of the Shetland Islands) and south about (via the North Sea and English Channel).

8.2   To pass north of the Shetland Islands, the extensive offshore oil installations to the north-east present navigational hazards.   The winter season weather further north is generally more severe and, at the time of BRAER's passage, the conditions would have been considerably worse due to the longer fetch of the southerly gales.   Since this route would necessarily have had to pass north of the offshore oil fields, there would have been no saving in distance, in fact it would have been 20 miles longer.

8.3   The southern North Sea and the English Channel are perhaps the busiest areas of water in the world.   Except for the western English Channel, there are numerous shoals which, although adequately marked, are a threat to any large vessel drifting without power.   Use of this route by BRAER would have meant the vessel initially heading directly into the weather on her passage down the North Sea.   She would have made minimum headway and possibly would have had to heave to.   The route would have also added 460 miles to the usual distance.

8.4   The northern Fair Isle Strait is 20 miles wide and the southern Strait is 22 miles wide.   Both have deep water and neither has any navigational hazards.   Although accurate figures are not available it has been estimated that each year some 1,400 laden tankers use the Straits, 70% of which are through vessels not putting in to Sullom Voe.   It has also been estimated that the total vessel movements in the Straits are less than 5% of those in the Dover Strait.   The Fair Isle Straits are a recognised channel for vessels between Northern Europe and North America and in the light of this IMO have agreed, on the recommendation of the UK Government, a recommended route through them.   It is therefore considered that the Master was justified in taking the route through the northern Fair Isle Strait as it is the least hazardous and the shortest one.   It is also an internationally recognised strait.

9.   CONTAMINATION OF THE DIESEL FUEL

9.1   It is highly likely that the loose pipes damaged a number of air pipes, including the aft one to the port double bottom diesel oil tank, allowing sea water to enter the tanks and spaces below. However, it does not necessarily follow that this damage occurred prior to, and was the sole cause of, the water contamination of the diesel fuel. It is also unclear as to how many air pipes were actually seen to be damaged on the afternoon of 4 January.

It has already been suggested that on the evidence available, the probability is that damage to these air pipes did occur, thus allowing the entry of sea water to the port double bottom diesel oil tank. As to the time at which that damage occurred, it is likely that sea water had entered the port double bottom diesel oil tank sometime after the settling tank had been 'topped up' during the 0800 hrs to 1200 hrs watch on 4 January. If the damage had occurred at an earlier time, excessive water discharge from the diesel oil purifier would have been sighted by the engine room watchkeepers whilst 'topping up' the service tank during the 2000 hrs to 2400 hrs watch on 4 January, prior to refilling the settling tank from the double bottom tanks.

9.2   Considering the diesel oil transfer routine on board BRAER, the normal diesel oil consumption whilst at sea was sufficiently low to require 'topping up' of the settling tank from the double bottom storage tanks only once every 12 hours, during the 8 to 12 watch. This routine is recorded in the engine log book from departure on 3 January until the 2000 hrs to 2400 hrs watch on 4 January.

These diesel oil movements, between the settling tank and the service tank via the purifier and also from the double bottom tanks to the settling tank, can be quantified by simple calculations using the service tank contents recorded per watch in the engine log book. These give the following quantities:

3 January

0400-0800 hrs	0.7 tonnes added to Service Tank
1200 hrs	Vessel departs Mongstad
2000-2400 hrs	1.0 tonnes added to Service Tank

4 January

0800-1200 hrs	1.1 tonnes added to Service Tank
2000-2400 hrs	1.3 tonnes added to Service Tank

The amount of diesel oil actually transferred from the double bottom tanks to the settling tank was not shown in the engine log book. However, it is understood that the diesel oil purifier was normally only operated on the 8 to 12 watch. This is the probable reason for a static level of 9.6 tonnes in the settling tank being recorded in the log book during the other watches.

9.3   Taking account that the log book showed that 1.3 tonnes was added to the service tank during the 2000 hrs to 2400 hrs watch on 4 January, that the diesel generator would have consumed 0.68 tonnes during that period and the main engine consumption for the half hour period before midnight would have been 1.1 tonnes a figure of 3.08 tonnes is arrived at. To this total must be added the amount of water that was being discharged from the purifier during the purification process. As the watchkeepers did not notice any unusual discharge the 3.08 tonnes can be rounded up to 3.1 tonnes to give the maximum amount transferred from the double bottom tanks to the settling tanks. If it is assumed that the air pipe for the port double bottom diesel oil tank was not sufficiently damaged to allow the entry of sea water until the afternoon of 4 January, then with suction from both double bottom tanks it would not be unreasonable to conclude that only about 1.6 tonnes would be taken from the port double bottom tank during that watch. With the total 3.1 tonnes added to the existing settling tank contents, any "free" water would be mixed throughout the tank contents delaying effective separation. Some free water would be drained out, but the bulk of the remaining mixture would then be passed through the diesel oil purifier.

The estimated dimensions of the diesel oil settling and service tanks suggest that each tank was approximately 2.5m x 1.5m x 3.0m, giving a capacity of about 11.5 tonnes each. Assuming that the entire 1.6 tonnes taken from the port double bottom tank was sea water, this would eventually occupy the lower part of the settling tank to a height of about 500mm. With little, or ineffective, usage of the drain valve owing to insufficient settling time and vessel movement, it is probable that water would enter the boiler diesel oil supply line (which fed the boiler directly from the settling tanks) as well as the purifier supply line. This scenario could account for the initial presence of sea water in the diesel oil supply line to the auxiliary boiler.

9.4   The presence of sea water in the diesel oil service tank requires consideration. No difficulties were recorded in operating the purifier, the required output being apparently well within its capacity and there is no record of the water seal failure alarm sounding. This therefore suggests that any sea water that had entered the diesel oil settling tank was being successfully removed by the diesel oil purifier during transfer to the service tank. The motorman on the 2000 hrs to 2400 hrs watch on the evening of 4 January did not notice any unusual discharge from the purifier, although the 0000 hrs to 0400 hrs watch motorman on the morning of 5 January did;

39

he had apparently seen nothing unusual during the early part of his watch but noted that during his rounds at about 0400 hrs there was an unusually large amount of water being discharged from the sludge pipe.

As the settling tank had been drained frequently since midnight by various members of the engine room staff, including the Chief Engineer, and it had been confirmed that the purifier was operating correctly, it is considered unlikely that the level of water found in the service tank could have originated only from damage to the aft air pipe of the port double bottom diesel oil tank.

9.5   The contents of the diesel oil service tank require consideration. At midnight on 4 January the service tank, from which the main engine (since 2330 hrs) and the diesel generator were drawing their fuel, was shown in the log book as containing 11.5 tonnes of diesel fuel, or about 100% tank capacity. The Third Engineer had re-started the diesel oil purifier at about 2330 hrs and confirmed that at about midnight the purifier was working correctly. At midnight, therefore, the quality of the diesel oil in the service tank would either:

-      not change, assuming no addition of water, or

-      deteriorate if water was added, eventually giving rise to a fuel/water emulsion.

The log book records that at 0400 hrs on 5 January the diesel oil service tank contained 5.8 tonnes of fuel. With the service tank contents being recorded as 11.5 tonnes at midnight, these figures would appear to show that the combined consumption of the main engine and diesel generator for the four hour period between midnight and 0400 hrs was 5.7 tonnes plus the input from the purifier and the loss from drainage. In the normal course of events, with the main engine running at about 106 rpm and one diesel generator operating, the calculated combined fuel consumption should be in the order of 9.5 tonnes. It follows therefore that assuming no significant entry of sea water but allowing for approximately one tonne to have been lost due to the draining process, the output of the diesel oil purifier would be in the order of 4.8 tonnes, that is 1.2 tonnes per hour.

The Alfa Laval diesel oil purifier installed on BRAER was a type MAPX 207 with a maximum output of 5750 litres/hour when purifying diesel oil of 14 cSt at 14 °C. Although this purifier was actually installed during building with a reduced output of about 3000 litres/hour, equating to approximately 2.6 tonnes per hour, the estimated purifier output of 4.8 tonnes over a four hour period was well within the machine's capability. Bearing in mind that salt water was known to be present in the service tank from about 0300 hrs the only other possible source of entry must have been via the air pipe.

9.6   The contents of the diesel oil settling tank are now considered. This tank is recorded as having 9.6 tonnes within it at midnight on 4 January. The Superintendent stated that at around 0300 hrs, he noted the contents as about 8 tonnes. A reduction of 1.6 tonnes over a 3 hour period during which the diesel oil purifier was operating and both the boiler supply line and the settling tank were being drained, suggests that the settling tank was being "topped up" from another source.

This calculation suggests that salt water was entering the settling tank in substantial quantities and as no diesel oil was or had been transferred from the double bottom diesel oil storage tanks after midnight, the source of entry must also have been via the air pipe.

9.7   Study of BRAER's plans and information from two sister vessels shows that the combined air pipe from the diesel oil settling and service tanks was fitted on the upper deck starboard side, adjacent to the accommodation block side bulkhead (see Figure 4). The height of the air pipe head is 760mm above the deck on one sister vessel and 970mm above the deck on the other (see Figure 7).

It is therefore reasonable to conclude that the combined settling and service tank air pipe on BRAER was on the upper deck (weather deck), on the starboard side, as was the case with the two sister vessels. Whether its height was the same as that of the other air pipes, or it had been extended as in the case of one of the sister vessels, is not known. The air pipe (which was common to both tanks) led down through the upper deck to the 1st platform deck immediately above the cylinder oil storage tanks. From there it passed inboard before turning forward to pass over the top of the settling and service tanks, the final connection being the service tank. In the engine room a drain line was fitted to the air pipe. This was a 15mm diameter line with a 'U' bend to act as a water and oil trap. This line drained down into the drip tray for the diesel tanks.

The weather during the whole passage from Mongstad had been on BRAER's port side, for some of the time it was abeam with the vessel reported as rolling up to 22°. The air pipe for the diesel oil service and settling tanks, being on the starboard side, would have been somewhat sheltered by the accommodation block. With the heavy rolling, however, large quantities of sea water would have been moving about the decks and it is possible that this air pipe could have been occasionally submerged in sea water.

The design of the float seal valve heads fitted to all the oil tank air pipes is such that under these conditions the valve should close, preventing the entry of water. However these valves are rarely totally weathertight and it would not be unusual for some water to gain entry. Normally any water would be drained away via the 15mm drain line fitted to the 80mm air pipe

41

and then into the drip tray surrounding the settling and service tanks. This in turn is led down to the 0.5 tonne capacity drain tank situated at the bottom of the engine room on the tank top.

The above scenario does however assume that the air pipe itself is intact and that the float valve is present, undamaged and with the valve seat free of debris. The absence of a float or significant damage to the pipe or its fittings would allow, under the circumstances of this accident, considerable volumes of water to enter the diesel oil settling and service tanks. In the event that the drain line became blocked or choked due to the ingress of large quantities of water, the water would back up and flow further down the air pipe until it entered initially the diesel oil settling and later the service tanks. Under this latter condition, the diesel oil in those tanks would become contaminated and would continue so even with liberal use of the drain valves fitted to both tanks.

9.8   A further alternative scenario as to the source of sea water contamination in the diesel oil service tank ought to be considered. With all crew efforts being concentrated on removing sea water from the settling tank the effect of the main engine consumption on the service tank contents might have been overlooked. If so, at approximately 0400 hrs on 5 January at the change of watch, the need to rapidly fill the tank would have been noted and the service tank could have been filled direct from the double bottom diesel oil tanks. As suction from the port double bottom tank would probably by now discharge pure sea water, such an action would add tonnes of sea water direct into the service tank. This would be followed very shortly afterwards by the ingress of water into the diesel fuel lines to both the main engine and the generators.

The Third Assistant Engineer stated that he instructed his motorman to put the diesel oil purifier back on at about 2330 hrs and that at midnight he confirmed that it was working. The First Assistant Engineer also confirmed that at about 0400 hrs he was told by his motorman that the diesel oil purifier was working. On the basis of these statements and the lack of any contradictory evidence, this alternative scenario has been discounted.

9.9   It has been suggested in some quarters that the problem with the diesel oil was not contamination by sea water but that the quality of the fuel supplied to the vessel was well below specification. The vessel had taken on diesel oil in New York in December 1992; samples of the oil were not available to the Inspectors. However, because no problems had been encountered with the generators or main engine running on diesel oil until the night of the incident this possibility is discounted.

10. ENGINE FAILURE

10.1 In early January the steam demand would have been relatively high due to an ambient air temperature varying between 5 and 8°C and a sea temperature of 9°C. On departure, the vessel experienced severe southerly gales with the result that the main engine revolutions were reduced to 89 rpm or 38.8% power output. This low power output would preclude effective use of the exhaust gas economiser as a steam generator. The main engine revolutions were increased to 106 rpm at 2000 hrs on 4 January; even so, the auxiliary boiler was still required to satisfy the steam demand.

10.2 At 2030 hrs on 4 January the Third Assistant Engineer, noticed that the high and low level boiler water alarms were sounding with unusual frequency as the water level fluctuated between the two alarm and trip points. He therefore decided to change the air transmitter which controls both alarms. As this procedure would affect control of the boiler water level, it was necessary to temporarily shut down the auxiliary boiler. Prior to shutting down, the fuel oil supply was changed to diesel oil supplied from the settling tank so as to facilitate easy re-starting of the boiler. This procedure is not unusual as any fuel oil left in the supply lines to the burner after shut down suffers heat loss, with a consequential rise in its viscosity and difficulty in subsequent ignition.

10.3 The boiler was eventually shut down at 2100 hrs to enable the apparently defective air transmitter to be changed for the spare unit. Whilst shut down, a minor problem developed but this was solved by draining the air supply lines. At 2230 hrs, the boiler start sequence was initiated, utilising the timed program for a cold boiler start. The steam pressure by this time had dropped to 3 kg/cm² in spite of the input from the main engine exhaust economiser. Moreover, during the period that the auxiliary boiler had been shut down steam heating was still being used for both domestic and main engine fuel oil heating purposes.

10.4 The main engine oil fuel temperature had by this time dropped to 95°C whereas the normal required fuel rail temperature was 118°C. This reduction in temperature, if allowed to continue, could have led to blockage of the filters due to high viscosity, bad combustion and fuel injection system wear. The correct decision was therefore made to change the main engine from heavy fuel to diesel and instructions were given to re-start the diesel oil purifier so as to maintain a safe level in the diesel oil service tank. From approximately midnight, therefore, both the main engine (operating at about 106 rpm) and the diesel generator were running on diesel oil supplied from the diesel oil service tank.

43

10.5   Although direct firing of the auxiliary boiler had been stopped the boiler water circulating pump continued to operate, passing the boiler water through the exhaust gas economiser and back to the auxiliary boiler steam drum. Given that the boiler had only been shut down for approximately one hour and that during this period steam, albeit at a low pressure, was still being generated, the selection of a warming through start-up sequence could be considered as an over cautious action by the Third Assistant Engineer. Efforts by the Third and subsequently the Second Assistant Engineer to fire the boiler on diesel oil continued until approximately 0030 hrs on 5 January when salt water was discovered in the diesel oil supply line from the settling tank to the burner.

10.6   This discovery by the Second Assistant Engineer was the first indication that contaminated fuel was present and that the firing problem may not have been due to an ignition or a firing control defect. Despite this discovery, the flame igniter was then tested and the boiler burner changed. The former test was successful whilst the latter had no discernable effect on the firing attempts. This suggests that at this time the Second Assistant Engineer was still not certain that water contaminated fuel was the problem.

10.7   During the whole period following the discovery of the water contamination all efforts had been concentrated on draining water from the diesel fuel in the settling tank and, to a lesser extent, from the service tank. These efforts were not successful and it resulted in the main engine and then the generator both stopping due to contaminated fuel, resulting in the disablement of the vessel.

10.8   Some considerable time after the grounding and after the vessel had broken up, divers surveyed the remains of the wreck. Their survey included a number of photographs which showed the scavenge case doors to be detached from the main engine. This led to a number of assertions that the engineers had been carrying out repairs to the main engine at the time of the incident.

There is no evidence to support this claim. Although there is no doubt that the photographs do show the scavenge doors to be detached from the main engine, the photographs clearly show that the whole engine room had broken up due to the actions of the sea: little if any of the machinery remains intact. The detachment of the scavenge doors would have been due to the actions of the sea alone and not because they had been removed by the vessel's engineers.

11. ACTIONS OF THE WATCHKEEPING ENGINEERS

11.1   The action of the Third Assistant Engineer in carrying out corrective maintenance work on the water level pneumatic controls of the boiler falls within the parameters of normal watchkeeping duties. A fault had manifested itself and he took the proper action in changing the boiler fuel from heavy oil to diesel oil prior to shut down. This action allowed him to undertake the necessary work and then re-fire the boiler on diesel oil.

11.2   The sequence of events that evolved within the engine room has two separate phases - the malfunction of a boiler water level alarm transmitter leading to a repair sequence and, secondly, the build-up of sea water within the diesel oil settling and service tanks.

11.3   The original fault and the subsequent minor defect have not been firmly established; there is a suggestion that the air pressure transmitter controlling the water level alarms was incorrectly set and that the low level alarm transmitter had a fault. Given that the latter fault was corrected by draining the air line, it would not be unreasonable to suggest that both faults may well have had their origin in the water contaminated air supply. If so, it suggests that either the air dryer installed in the system supply line was less than efficient or the air bottles were not being drained regularly.

11.4   The other three major decisions by the Third Assistant Engineer, namely re-starting the auxiliary boiler using the timed firing sequence, changing the main engine fuel from heavy oil to diesel oil and re-starting the diesel oil purifier were correct under the circumstances prevailing at the time. With hindsight, it would have been prudent to ensure that non-essential steam lines were shut off at an early stage to conserve the steam pressure as high as possible for the essential service, of the heating of the fuel oil. At the time, however, there was no reason for the Third Assistant Engineer to anticipate a re-firing problem. Under normal circumstances the re-firing of the boiler would rapidly restore the proper boiler steam pressure and all would have been well.

11.5   The Second Assistant Engineer did identify water in the fuel as the principal problem, this discovery being made at approximately 0030 hrs on 5 January. However, despite having established by taste that the contamination was sea water, no apparent attempt was made to establish where this water was coming from. This officer should have known that there were only two possible sources of sea water entry: either from the double bottom tanks when the settling tank was topped up during the previous 8 to 12 watch or via the air pipe from the upper deck.

11.6   Confirmation of the possible entry point could and should have been established by checking the quality of the diesel fuel in both the settling and service tanks. Assuming no diesel oil purifier alarms had sounded, testing for water via the drain valve on the service tank would have indicated water entry by way of the tank air pipe system. Further evidence could have been obtained by examining the output from the air pipe drain line. The evidence suggests that neither of these tests were carried out by the Second Assistant Engineer. It seems that he did not appreciate the significance of the presence of sea water and concentrated his efforts on attempting to fire the boiler rather than establish the source of the water contamination.

11.7   It should be noted that if the Third Assistant Engineer had chosen not to carry out any repair work on the boiler water pneumatic system the boiler and main engine would have continued to run on heavy fuel and the vessel would have continued to operate until such time as the sea water contaminated diesel oil in the service tank affected the running of the generator, when a 'blackout' would have occurred. It is not possible to predict when this 'blackout' would have occurred; but there is no question that it would have happened sooner or later. Whether the consequence of such a 'blackout' would have resulted in the vessel going aground is equally unpredictable.

12. ACTIONS OF CHIEF ENGINEER AND SUPERINTENDENT

12.1   The Chief Engineer's action in authorising the Third Assistant Engineer to change the main engine fuel from heavy oil to diesel due to the steam heating problems was correct, although it is unusual that he did not apparently enquire what the problem was. It may be that knowing the Second Assistant Engineer was shortly to take over the watch and that his special responsibility was the steam plant, he felt that the problem could be safely left to that officer.

12.2   When eventually called down to the engine room at about 0230 hrs, the Chief Engineer correctly diagnosed water contaminated fuel in both the diesel oil settling and service tanks. As he would have been aware that the watchkeepers efforts since 0030 hrs had been concentrated on removing water from the diesel oil supply, it is surprising he did not attempt to establish the point of entry of the contaminating sea water. Again all efforts were concentrated on draining water from the fuel - no attempt was made to establish the source of sea water entry. With some three hours having elapsed since the first attempts to re-fire the boiler, and with sea water still being found in the diesel fuel, it should have been obvious to the Chief Engineer that the ingress of sea water was continuing. Furthermore as no additional diesel fuel had been pumped up from the double bottom tanks, the sea water must have had another point of entry.

12.3   The Superintendent, on entering the engine room at about 0200 hrs, noted that problems were being experienced with water contaminated fuel at the boiler front, and after about half an hour advised the Second Assistant Engineer to call out the Chief Engineer. For the next one and a half hours the Superintendent assisted the Second Assistant Engineer in attempting to fire the boiler and with the Chief Engineer checked on the draining of the settling and service tanks. Whilst it is appreciated that the Chief Engineer was responsible for the vessel's technical operation, the Superintendent was the Company's senior technical man on board, and it would be reasonable to expect him to have become more involved in <u>analysing</u> the problem.

12.4   It is apparent that neither the Chief Engineer nor the Superintendent checked the air pipe drain line. Neither did they carry out a preliminary check of the diesel oil settling and service tank levels to establish how effective the draining process was or whether sea water was entering from another source.

Given the weather conditions, no action could have been taken on deck unless the vessel hove to. It has also been suggested that the height clearance between the diesel oil settling and service tanks and the deck head was insufficient to allow the air pipes to be disconnected. An examination of a sister vessel showed that there are bolted flanges adjacent to each tank entry plus a further one just clear of the tank structure. The height clearance between the top of the tank and the deckhead was approximately one metre. There is no doubt that the air pipe within the engine room spaces could have been isolated.

12.5   The draining of fuel lines and other remedial measures should have been well within the capabilities of the watchkeeping staff, leaving both the Chief Engineer and the Superintendent free to analyse the situation and prepare a suitable course of action. Unfortunately neither seemed to be able to look beyond the immediate situation and consider the broader question as to the source of sea water entry.

12.6   It is not known whether the contents of the starboard double bottom diesel oil tank were contaminated by sea water. The two air pipes for that tank terminated on the starboard side of the upper deck, and, despite what has been said earlier at section 6.18, it is possible that these might not have been damaged. When transferring fuel from the double bottom to the settling tank suction was taken from both the port and starboard double bottom diesel oil tanks but this is unlikely to have allowed water contamination from the port tank to enter the starboard tank. It is possible therefore that the fuel in the starboard double bottom diesel oil tank was not contaminated. If the Chief Engineer and the Superintendent had given early and proper consideration to the source of seawater entry into the diesel oil settling and service tanks and also considered the possibility of the starboard double bottom diesel oil tank being uncontaminated the following chain of events might have been possible: disconnection of the air pipe to the settling and service tanks; setting up the service tank into a closed circuit purification system (service tank - purifier - service tank); completely draining the settling tank (this would have to be into the bilges as the dump line drains into the starboard double bottom diesel oil tank); replenishing the settling tank with uncontaminated diesel oil from the starboard double bottom tank; reverting to the normal system of diesel oil from the settling tank to the purifier then to the service tank which, by that stage due to the closed circuit purification system, would have contained less contaminated diesel oil. During this whole operation it would be necessary to stop the main engine to conserve the quantity of diesel oil in the service tank and the Master would have to be consulted and his approval given to stop the main engines for possibly up to two hours. If, of course, the closed circuit purification system had not resulted in an improved quality of diesel oil in the service tank the diesel generator would have stopped, the vessel would have no power and the attempts would have been to no avail. However, if the attempt had been successful the main engines could then be restarted on diesel oil in sufficient time to prevent the vessel going aground, the boiler firing sequence successfully completed and when the heavy fuel oil was at the required temperature the main engines changed over to heavy fuel. There is no guarantee this chain of actions would have been successful; a number of unknown factors might have come into play but it would have been worthy of consideration if proper thought had been given to the source of contamination at an early stage.

13.   ACTIONS OF MASTER

13.1   When the Master made visits to the bridge during 3 and 4 January, it seems unlikely that he went outside the wheelhouse during those visits. The Chief and Second Officers both said that they spent their entire watches inside the wheelhouse and it is highly likely that the Third Officer did the same. The Second Officer said that shortly after 1600 hrs on 3 January he sent one of his watch ratings to see if the port lifeboat was secure. The Chief Officer said that he did not send anybody down during his morning watch on 4 January (his first since leaving Mongstad). The Second Officer could not remember doing so on this day. It would therefore appear that no effort was made as part of the watchkeeper's duties to ensure that the spare pipes, oxygen and acetylene bottles and drums of hydraulic oil were secure.

13.2   The whole of BRAER's deck forward of the bridge was visible from within the wheelhouse. The only part of the after weather deck in view, looking through the after windows of the wheelhouse, was the area aft of the mooring winches. The deck forward of this, where the spare pipes were stowed, could not be seen from these windows. If an observer left the wheelhouse, went to the after end of the captain's deck and looked down, the whole of the weather deck abreast of the engine casing would have been clearly in view (see Figure 8). From within the accommodation, the port side of the engine casing (where the spare pipes had been secured) was visible from crew cabins on the bridge and upper bridge decks as well as from the crew messroom. There would have been no difficulty in making regular checks of the spare pipe stowage without going out on the weather deck. The oxygen and acetylene bottles and the drums of hydraulic oil could be observed from the various windows and ports across the after part of the boat deck accommodation and from the starboard windows of the officer's messroom, respectively.

13.3   The Master's instructions to his deck officers concerning regular checks to ensure that all was secure around the outside decks in heavy weather appear to be minimal. He stated that during the night he instructed the bridge officer on duty to shine the Aldis lamp around the accommodation from the bridge, about every twenty minutes. Both the Chief and Second Officers said they spent their entire watches inside the wheelhouse; it follows that either this instruction was not complied with or it was not made known to the officers.

13.4   The Master was aware of the sizes of the spare pipes because he had inspected them after the rack was constructed. It is therefore surprising that on being told they were loose, on the morning of 4 January, he did not even go to the crew messroom window to have a look at them. Neither did he tell anybody to keep him informed as to what damage they may have

49

been causing. The Chief Engineer said that he told the Master that the air pipes were being damaged. This has not been corroborated by anyone else, but even so the Master should have taken some interest in the matter. The loose pipes could be heard by the watchkeepers in the engine control room. If the bridge watchkeepers had occasionally left the wheelhouse for the outside bridge deck, they would probably have heard them. If they had gone to the port bridge wing in daylight and looked aft they would certainly have seen them. It is likely that the 'rumbling' of the pipes would have been heard from the officer's messroom as well as the crew messroom. There are invariably a variety of noises to be heard in any vessel in heavy weather, but a prudent seaman is usually attentive to noises which are unusual or unexpected.

13.5   The Master told the Superintendent, Chief Officer and Chief Engineer that nothing could be done about the pipes because of the severe weather conditions. On that particular course, with the vessel rolling heavily and shipping heavy seas from the port side, it was clearly out of the question to send the crew out to try to secure the pipes. However the Master could have thought about some other way of dealing with the problem. He should have considered heaving to with the weather on the starboard bow, to minimise the rolling and put the loose pipes in the lee of the accommodation house and engine casing. It is likely that it would then have been safe enough to send men out to that relatively sheltered part of the deck. Re-securing the pipes sufficiently well to withstand a resumption of the passage in those weather conditions would have been extremely difficult, and consideration to jettisoning them might have been preferable; there would have been little difficulty in cutting a gap in the side rails, should this have been necessary, to facilitate the jettisoning. In the event the Master did nothing which suggests a fundamental lack of basic seamanship.

When the Superintendent called him at about 0410 hrs and reported water in the diesel oil tanks, one would have expected the Master to wonder how this could have happened. If he had done so, he would perhaps have remembered the loose pipes having been reported to him the previous morning. It seems that this did not occur to the Master, or to anybody else.

13.6   The failure of the Master to request a tug immediately after the power failure occurred can perhaps be excused. He was relying on the advice of the Superintendent, who apparently thought that there was still a chance of draining the contaminated fuel and restoring power. The Master realised that his vessel was drifting downwind, but there was no certainty at that early stage that she would fetch up on lower Shetland, a narrow peninsula of land ten miles to the north.

At 0526 hrs, when he was in contact with Shetland Coastguard, the Master did make it very clear that he required a tug as soon as possible. The Coastguard's reaction to this request is discussed in Section 14. However the Master should then have backed up his call for a tug with an Urgency message to all stations, when it was evident to him that the Coastguard had not done so. On the other hand, he had perhaps gained the impression from Shetland Coastguard that a suitable tug was available in Lerwick. On balance, although BRAER's emergency power was limited, the Master should have made an Urgency call for a tug to all stations, on both HF and VHF.

The Merchant Shipping (Reporting of Pollution Incidents) Regulations 1987 require the Master of any ship involved in an incident at sea within United Kingdom territorial waters, involving a probable discharge of oil, to report the incident. It appears that the information provided to Shetland Coastguard during the Master's conversation with them at 0526 hrs satisfied these Regulations.

13.7   As BRAER continued to drift, the Master told Shetland Coastguard that the rate of drift could not be determined because there was no power to operate the navigational equipment. However, the magnetic compass is capable of being used to take bearings, as well as steer by. Sumburgh Head Light, with a range of 23 miles, is known to have been visible and Fair Isle Light, with a range of 22 miles, would also have been well within range. It should have been possible to take visual cross bearings using these lights; in fact Shetland Coastguard asked for this to be done. Although the vessel was rolling heavily and the spread between the bearings would not have been the most ideal for an accurate fix, the fixes obtained would have given an adequate estimation of the direction and rate of drift. If Fair Isle Light was not visible from BRAER, then a succession of bearings of Sumburgh Head Light, if they showed no appreciable change, would have given a good indication that BRAER was likely to fetch up ashore.

13.8   The agreement to declare an Urgency situation and evacuate 16 non-essential crew when BRAER was about four miles south of Sumburgh Head was a correct one, although the suggestion that it was time to take these actions should have come from the Master rather than the Coastguard. So far as the Master was concerned there is no criticism of the way this crew muster and evacuation was carried out, apparently without panic and without any injuries. Similarly, there can be no criticism of the Master's decision to finally abandon BRAER, albeit a decision urged upon him by one of the rescue units.

14.   ACTIONS OF HM COASTGUARD AND RESCUE SERVICES

14.1   At Shetland Coastguard, watch is kept in the Operations Room by the Senior Watch Officer (SWO) and two Watch Officers (WOs). Each officer is seated at an individual console from which he or she can use all the means of communication, including VHF radio and telephones. On receipt or transmission of a communication, by whatever means, the officer concerned types a brief summary of it into the Data Acquisition System. Entries into this system are each preceded by the time of entry and the officer's initials and the entries can be viewed on the VDU screens at all three consoles. The SWO usually handles individual communications himself, according to circumstances, but he also exercises overall supervision of the watch. He can do this by listening through his headset to another officer's communications, speaking directly to another officer or looking at the entered data on the VDU screen. During an incident, all significant events should be brought to the SWO's attention; he makes decisions on actions to be taken, such as the alerting or tasking of the various rescue services. In the course of any incident the SWO may at his discretion alert the Duty District Officer (DDO), who may be the District Controller (DC) or one of his senior non-watchkeeping officers. The arrival of the DDO in the Operations Room does not necessarily mean that he will take immediate active charge of the incident, but he will monitor what is happening and responsibilities for decisions will devolve to him.

On the morning of the incident, a qualified Watch Officer was substituting for the Senior Watch Officer who was on leave and the other two Watch Officers were a new entry probationary Coastguard and an auxiliary.

14.2   The prime role of HM Coastguard in any emergency situation is to co-ordinate search and rescue actions with the aim of saving life. However, it has been the practice for Coastguard to try to obtain towage (or other assistance) for a vessel whose crew are in no immediate danger, if so requested by her master. Any commercial agreement for such assistance is strictly a matter between the Master or owners and the assisting vessel. The Coastguard should not become a party to commercial towage or salvage operations and emergency towing is rarely necessary, or even possible, as a means of saving life. They may however relay communications.

14.3   The first VHF conversation between the Master of BRAER and Shetland Coastguard which commenced at 0526 hrs, some 45 minutes after the engine failure, concerned the need for both helicopter assistance and towage assistance. The Master said he did not require helicopter assistance but asked for towage assistance. The Coastguard, mindful of their prime duty to ensure there was no loss of life, commenced arrangements for the helicopter to be alerted, but the matter of towage was less clear as can be seen from the following extracts, over a period of two minutes, from the transcript:

52

BRAER:	I require only tugboat for towing ... because we have not engine ... we require the towing as soon as possible because we are laden condition we have full load crude oil.
CG:	(after querying position and drift) Do you wish us to contact the Harbour Authorities in Lerwick and ask them to provide a tug for your assistance?
BRAER:	OK thank you very much.
CG:	Are your owners willing to pay the commercial rate for this towage?
BRAER:	I don't know ... I don't know if you can make arrange for the tug because just now I haven't contacted with my owners ...
CG:	We will pre-warn the Harbour of the likelihood that you require a tug. It will take two hours maybe three to get down to where you are.

14.4 The Master, having made a clear and repeated request for towage, became confused by the Coastguard question concerning payment and evidently came to the conclusion that towage would not be provided without prior agreement involving his owners. It seems surprising, bearing in mind the request for a tug "as soon as possible", that the Coastguard did not explain that they are not concerned with commercial matters. Equally, the Master being aware of the position he was in, should not have allowed himself to be confused by the Coastguard query. On the immediate need for towage, Coastguard had every means of communication at their disposal to relay the Master's request for towage assistance throughout the area. It is fair to say that such a request from Coastguard could not have been given an Urgency prefix because the Master had not declared a PAN PAN (Urgency) situation. However, the local telephone calls made by Coastguard to 'pre-warn of the likelihood' that tugs would be needed did not have any real sense of urgency to them. It is clear from the full tape transcripts that there were language difficulties experienced during a number of the VHF and telephone conversations with the Master; this one was no exception. Also, radio reception was poor and transmissions from BRAER kept "breaking". This first conversation with BRAER spanned a period, with breaks and interruptions, of nearly five and a half minutes. During the opening phases of the incident co-ordination of the rescue placed a heavy workload on the three Coastguard watchkeepers. This, combined with the language problem and the poor radio reception, may explain why the local telephone calls for tugs lacked a sense of urgency.

14.5   Consideration has to be given to the likelihood or otherwise of a different outcome of the accident, had Coastguard immediately relayed BRAER's firm request for towage, say at 0530 hrs, by HF and VHF broadcasts to 'all stations' as well as by telephone calls. There were two sources of suitable towage assistance and one possible source. The two which are known were the tugs SWAABIE and TIRRICK at Sullom Voe and STAR SIRIUS at Lerwick, all of which were dispatched some time later in the incident. The possible source is the chance, albeit a remote one, that another suitable vessel might have been in the area at the time, either at sea or manned and keeping a radio watch in harbour.

14.6   The Sullom Voe tugs are intended for the handling of large tankers. SWAABIE and TIRRICK had engine powers of 3,800 and 4,000 bhp with bollard pulls of 54 and 45 tonnes respectively, and they also carried equipment for sea towage. SWAABIE started to prepare for sea at 0600 hrs, having heard about BRAER through Sullom Voe Port Control. Ten minutes later the confirmed request for a tug was passed by Coastguard to Port Control, who relayed it to Shetland Towage Ltd, the tugs' owners. The necessary preparations for sea included the calling in of two extra deckhands and the replacement of harbour towing gear with the sea towing gear from its below-deck stowage. These preparations, initially without the extra deckhands, took until 0815 hrs, when SWAABIE put to sea, followed later by TIRRICK. The distance to BRAER was 52 miles by the inside route, passing west of Whalsay Island and through Lerwick Harbour. The tugs therefore had the benefit of some shelter during the initial part of the passage and achieved speeds of about 9 knots, into a Force 7 to 9 southerly wind with a high swell. By the time BRAER grounded SWAABIE and TIRRICK were passing through Lerwick Harbour, with more than 20 miles still to go.

14.7   Once clear of Lerwick Harbour SWAABIE and TIRRICK would have been in open sea for the rest of the passage and the best possible average speed they could have made good would have been 8 knots. In the words of the General Manager of Shetland Towage, "even this speed would have been an ambitious estimate". The preparations for sea had been made as quickly as possible, in the light of the confirmed request for a tug. The best passage time would have been about seven hours and the tugs could not have arrived at BRAER until mid-afternoon. If a firm request for towage had been relayed by Coastguard at 0530 hrs, the earliest possible time of arrival of the Sullom Voe tugs at BRAER would probably have been 1400 hrs.

14.8   STAR SIRIUS is an anchor handling/tug supply vessel with a continuous bollard pull of 110 tonnes. She was lying alongside a berth at Holmsgarth (one mile from Lerwick) after discharging cargo from an offshore installation. The vessel was fully manned although, as is customary for a vessel berthed safely in port, her radio installation was closed down. Shetland Coastguard first contacted Lerwick Port Control and discussed towage at 0534 hrs, straight after their first conversation with BRAER. At this time no mention was made of the presence in port of STAR SIRIUS.

14.9 Lerwick Port Control later made two telephone calls to Shetland Coastguard, at 0556 hrs and again at 0603 hrs. Both conversations included discussion about the availability of suitable tugs. It was during the second conversation that Coastguard was told that STAR SIRIUS was in the port and might be made available. The WO who took this call typed an entry in the Data Acquisition System at 0604 hrs. The entry read "Fm Lwk Port Control We have no tug big enough should one be required but there is a tug at Holmsgarth "Star Sirius" which may be available fm (charterers name given)". At 0623 hrs Coastguard again asked Lerwick Port Control about the availability of their own tugs. Port Control again suggested that STAR SIRIUS could be made available. Coastguard asked if the vessel could be requested to contact them.

14.10 The Lerwick Duty Pilot went aboard STAR SIRIUS, woke her Master, briefed him on the situation and asked if his vessel could render immediate assistance to BRAER. The Master agreed. The vessel was at the time rigged for her role as a supply vessel and, although the deck was clear of cargo, it was necessary to open the stern gates and prepare for towage. STAR SIRIUS sailed at 0710 hrs. Once clear of Lerwick Harbour the propeller speed had to be reduced by 25% due to the weather. The Master reported the wind as south-by-east force 8 to 9, occasionally gusting to force 10 with heavy snow showers. At 0938 hrs STAR SIRIUS arrived at BRAER, which was abandoned and drifting one mile SSE of Horse Island. STAR SIRIUS had reached BRAER in two and a half hours at an average speed of nearly nine knots.

14.11 If Coastguard could have passed the request for towage directly to STAR SIRIUS at 0530 hrs, then the earliest time she could have arrived at BRAER would have been 0830 hrs. At this time the Master of BRAER had accepted the advice of helicopter R137 to abandon ship and evacuation of the remaining crew had just started. BRAER was reported as half a mile south-east of Horse Island and then thought to be in imminent danger of grounding. Looking at the situation as it then was, and with the benefit of hindsight, it has to be considered whether or not the outcome would have been any different if STAR SIRIUS had been there at that time. It is possible that a towline could have been connected before BRAER went aground, had adequate assistance to do this been available on the vessel. However, at 0830 hrs all the indications were that BRAER would continue to drift downwind and ground very shortly, either on Horse Island or in West Voe. When this happened there was a danger of a rapid break up of the hull, together with the possibility of explosion and fire. In the event this did not happen, but with such dangers present evacuation of any crew remaining on board would have been extremely hazardous. On balance it would still have been a prudent decision to abandon BRAER, even if STAR SIRIUS had been standing by her at that time.

14.12   The first indications that BRAER was not going to ground as had been expected perhaps became apparent at 0905 hrs. If STAR SIRIUS had been on scene at that time and adequate crew could have been landed back on board BRAER then there would have been two hours available to connect a tow and hold her until the Sullom Voe tugs and other assistance arrived. There were two rescue helicopters available which would have provided continuous coverage on scene, since refuelling facilities were only minutes away. Evacuation could therefore have been achieved comparatively quickly if this was needed.

BRAER was not provided with any dedicated towlines. Very few vessels, especially ones of that size, are so equipped these days and it is customary to use towlines provided by the tug for harbour towage purposes. BRAER was equipped aft with three mooring winches and a total of six mooring wires and four mooring ropes, with new spare ropes stowed below deck in the steering gear compartment. Two of the mooring winches were aft of the engine casing (see Figure 4); each one was fitted with two drums on which were permanently rove mooring wires with nylon pennants connected to their outer ends by Mandel shackles. Four polypropylene 200mm circumference plaited mooring ropes, with a soft eye at each end, were also provided. When the vessel left port each rope was lightly lashed to one of the nylon pennants of the mooring wires and then wound on to the drum. The outer eyes were lightly secured and the drums then covered with canvas. Each drum was fitted with a band brake operated by a hand wheel and all the drums were left out of gear when the vessel was at sea. Forward of the bridge superstructure was a similar winch with two wires permanently rove on the drums.

Polypropylene mooring ropes have properties of being light in weight and easy to handle. Those on BRAER, if in good condition, would have had breaking stresses of about 40 tonnes. The band brakes on the two mooring winches were reported to be in good condition and easy to operate by one man. The wires were each 200m in length and 36mm in diameter, with a probable breaking stress of about 80 tonnes if in good condition. It should therefore have been feasible, within the two hours which would have been available, for a polypropylene rope and then a wire to be heaved across to STAR SIRIUS by her winch power, allowing it to run out under control using the band brake. If the procedure could have been repeated with one more of the remaining three sets of ropes and wires, then it must be considered possible that BRAER could have been held up into the weather until further assistance arrived, assuming that the winch brakes held and did not allow the wires to be pulled off the drums.

14.13　　The third and final possibility to consider is whether a suitable vessel in the area might have responded and proceeded to assist if Coastguard had relayed the request for towage assistance by HF and VHF to 'all ships' at 0530 hrs. Suitable vessels would include salvage tugs and large offshore vessels with towing capabilities, like STAR SIRIUS. Salvage tugs invariably keep a continuous radio watch on HF as well as VHF (particularly in extreme weather conditions) and BRAER's initial call on HF to Wick Radio, in which she described her predicament, would have been heard and almost certainly acted upon; similarly the first VHF communication with Shetland Coastguard, when she asked for a tug, would have brought an immediate response. However, the likelihood of a salvage tug or other large tug being in the immediate area must be discounted. The chances of an offshore vessel being at sea in the Fair Isle Strait or off the south part of Shetland on that night must be very small. The Fair Isle Strait is well away from the tracks taken by such vessels working the main offshore fields to the north-east and east of the Shetland Islands. Another offshore vessel might have been in the vicinity of Lerwick Harbour; if this had been so it is probable that she would have heard BRAER's VHF call for towage and, if she was in a position to do so, she would probably have responded to it.

14.14　　On balance, if Shetland Coastguard had immediately relayed 'to all stations' BRAER's request for a tug at 0530 hrs it is unlikely that the grounding would have been averted. Similarly, the twenty minute delay in the dispatch of STAR SIRIUS is also unlikely to have adversely affected the events which followed.

14.15　　There remains the question of whether adequate action was taken after the immediate threat of grounding had receded at 0915 hrs.

The Coastguard and the Marine Pollution Control Unit (MPCU) form the Marine Emergency Organisation (MEO) which is headed by the Director of Marine Emergency Operations (DMEO). If necessary to avoid serious pollution the DMEO may impose towage or other assistance on a vessel on behalf of the Secretary of State for Transport, who is given such powers under the Prevention of Oil Pollution Act 1971. The Act also gives powers for the taking of whatever direct action is necessary, which may include taking control of an abandoned vessel likely to cause serious pollution.

14.16　　The DC had arrived in the Coastguard Operations Room at about 0715 hrs and, after being briefed by the DDO, took overall charge of co-ordination actions. Some time later in the incident, the DMEO enquired as to whether or not BRAER had been asked to let go the anchors. It appears that the question of using the anchors had already been raised with BRAER, but there is no evidence of any definitive response.

At 0845 hrs, in a briefing from the DC, the DMEO was advised that it looked as if BRAER would not drift clear of the land and that the evacuation of the remaining crew was proceeding. At 0904 hrs the DMEO was told that the abandonment was complete and that STAR SIRIUS was expected to arrive between 0930 hrs and 1000 hrs. It was at about this time that it became apparent that BRAER was not going to ground as soon as had been expected. The DC realised that if people could be put on board, initially with the intention of trying to let go BRAER's anchors, a grounding might be averted, but this presented a dilemma. If men were put on board, the vessel might still go aground with the possibility of explosion and fire. Anyone going on board the vessel in such circumstances would be at grave risk and to put men at such risk in an operation which might not be a lifesaving one was totally contrary to the fundamental principles of the Coastguard. However, he balanced the need to do so against the gains which might be achieved and telephoned the Regional Controller (RC) (based at Aberdeen) at 0914 hrs and asked for his agreement to put the Master and some crew on board. The agreement was given, and it should then have been a matter of urgency to find volunteers and land them on board as soon as possible.

Once the Master and his crew had been evacuated by helicopter from BRAER they were landed at Sumburgh Airport and sent to the terminal building under the care of the Police, which was the usual procedure when survivors are landed ashore. Additionally, a Police Liaison Officer had been at Shetland Coastguard since 0709 hrs to assist with communications involving the Police, and this was carried out via a Police portable radio telephone. The Coastguard therefore had no direct communications with the Master which hampered their future efforts to discuss with him the possibility of himself and some crew members being returned to the vessel.

14.17   When the DC spoke to the RC at 0914 hrs STAR SIRIUS was only 25 minutes away from BRAER, yet nobody ashore appears to have considered what was to be done when she arrived. Even if crew could have been landed on the forecastle head, they could have done no more than try to let go the anchors. It appears that there was no shortage of volunteers to accompany the Master back to BRAER. It would perhaps have been logical to have considered trying to land crew at both ends of BRAER, so that one party could prepare for STAR SIRIUS and the other could attempt to release the anchors. Urgent consultation was also needed to decide how the tug was to be made fast. During a telephoned briefing at 0935 hrs the DMEO was told about the intention to land crew on BRAER's forecastle head and that STAR SIRIUS was nearly on scene. He observed that somebody would be needed on board anyway to take a line from the tug.

14.18   The Master of BRAER had told the DC that (in his opinion) the anchors could only be let go without the use of power in a depth of less than 30 metres. That was, perhaps, normal practice but this was not the time to be looking for ideal anchoring conditions and the immediate priority should have been to clear the cables and then try to get the anchors down from their housed positions; this in itself might not have been an easy task, since anchors sometimes tend not to run from the hawse pipe without prior 'walking out' under power. Once out of the hawse pipes the anchors may have been capable of being lowered in short and controlled stages.

14.19   In the event, the plan to lower volunteer crew on to BRAER's forecastle head had to be abandoned. (This was shortly after STAR SIRIUS arrived). The Pilot of helicopter R117, after assessing the possibilities, decided that the attempt would be too hazardous due to the close proximity of BRAER's foremast. It was now recognised that crew needed to be landed on the stern to assist the waiting STAR SIRIUS to set up a towline. The DC managed to get in telephone contact with the Master of BRAER at 1010 hrs, to explain his proposals.

14.20   Despite the misunderstandings due to language problems, it was eventually agreed with the Master that five crew and two marine pilots would be landed on the stern. The DC told the Master that he would get in touch with him again later, after organising the helicopter. It appears that key personnel became separated at the Airport and there were long delays while the Police gathered together the boarding party. It was at 1055 hrs that helicopter R117 finally lifted off for BRAER: a delay of 45 minutes. Sadly, these delays precluded effective action being taken to avoid the grounding.

14.21   It has already been pointed out that the prime role of the Coastguard is to co-ordinate search and rescue activities with the aim of saving life. This role effectively ceased at 0900 hrs when the rescue operation was successfully completed. At that time BRAER was very close inshore in West Voe and was expected to go aground within a few minutes. At that stage there could be no reasonable expectation that BRAER would remain afloat for another two hours or that STAR SIRIUS would arrive before she finally grounded. At about 0915 hrs reports received by the Coastguard indicated that BRAER was drifting out to sea. The DC then began planning to put people back on board, as described previously. As the Senior Coastguard "on-scene" he was in no doubt that it was his role to make and implement if possible any plan to prevent the vessel going aground. He had no explicit instructions from the DMEO on the action he should take. The DMEO had left it to the DC to take whatever actions were considered necessary because he (the DMEO) was remote from the scene and did not have a clear enough picture of what was happening.

The DC's authority was tacitly understood. He took the difficult decision to put people back on board the drifting ship initially with the aim of lowering the anchors. It is possible if clear instructions had been given that he would have appreciated the need to make arrangements to secure a tow line should STAR SIRIUS arrive soon enough.

Coastguard Standing Instructions did not explicitly give the Coastguard a duty to prevent a vessel going aground or foundering to avoid pollution. The actions to avoid pollution might encompass the arrangements for towage, and a possibility of placing people on board an abandoned vessel either to anchor it or to take a tow. This accident highlights the need for this important role of the Coastguard to be recognised and clearly set out. Towards this end, since the accident Coastguard Instructions have been amended and arrangements are being considered by DMEO to assist the provision of tugs to a disabled vessel. These arrangements are:

1. All Coastguard rescue centres will maintain an up-to-date database of all tugs in their areas, together with their capabilities, readiness and contact arrangements.

2. When a rescue centre receives information about a vessel broken down, or having suffered any other accident placing her or other vessels or offshore installations in jeopardy, Lloyds Intelligence will be informed immediately (after lifesaving action, if any, has been initiated). Lloyds will be asked to inform the co-ordinating Coastguard rescue centre of the response from those contacted.

3. The Senior Watch Officer will determine at the earliest opportunity the availability of the nearest tugs which might provide assistance. He will alert the vessels, brief their Masters and urge the Master of the casualty to employ them.

4. If the Master of the casualty refuses, prevaricates or fails to give any positive intention that he wishes tugs to attend, the Duty Regional Officer (DRO) will make a clear formal statement to the Master or owner that the Department will itself employ the tugs to stand-by on scene, and will seek to recover the costs from the owner or his insurers.

14.22   Section 14.15 refers to the Secretary of State's powers to direct the Master of a vessel, or to take direct action, to prevent pollution. These are sometimes known as the "intervention powers" because they derive from the 1969 International Intervention Convention. The use of these powers might have been necessary in this incident if the Master of BRAER had not been prepared to comply voluntarily with requests made to him by the Coastguard to prevent the vessel going aground. But that situation did not arise. The Intervention Powers are delegated by the Secretary of State to the DMEO but no further. The BRAER incident shows that the DMEO may not be close enough to the action, or have enough information, to be able to give explicit instructions for intervention in a fast-moving emergency.

The question arises of whether it should be possible for the DMEO to delegate the intervention powers further to a senior Department of Transport official on the spot. This did not affect the outcome of this particular accident but nevertheless such arrangements should be put in hand to cover future eventualities.

14.23   In this Section of the Report very little reference has been made about the actions taken by the Coastguard in carrying out their main role: co-ordination of rescue and preventing loss of life. Coastguard carried out this role in an exemplary manner and in the first few hours of the incident the three Coastguards on watch had to make not only the arrangements for the helicopters and brief their crews but also provide situation reports to the various authorities and respond to numerous other telephone calls which were being put through to them. For example, in the first 45 minutes of the incident 36 telephone calls were either made or received in addition to radio traffic. It is a credit to all concerned that the evacuation of the crew was successfully carried out: not only was there no loss of life but nobody suffered any injury. The bravery and skill of the two helicopter crews in the extreme weather conditions showed outstanding professionalism.

PART III   FURTHER COMMENT AND DISCUSSION

15.   EMERGENCY ANCHORING ARRANGEMENTS FOR LARGE TANKERS

15.1   BRAER had two independent anchor windlasses on her forecastle head, each provided with a conventional anchor and cable with the hawse pipes set at an angle of about 45° below the horizontal. When the vessel left Mongstad on 3 January the anchors were secured for sea in the usual way; the band brakes and cable compressors were applied, the cable lifters were out of gear, a chain lashing set up by a bottle screw was on each cable and the spurling pipes were closed with cover plates, sandbags, canvas and cement. Various members of the crew stated that the anchors could be cleared and let go by one or two men, without difficulty.

15.2   There is no doubt that BRAER had been frequently shipping seas across her weather deck, between the bridge and the forecastle head, for much of the passage. She continued to do so after the engine failure and for the entire period up to the grounding; this is very clear from the video film taken at the time. There was no sheltered access to the forecastle head, neither was there an elevated gangway or 'flying bridge'. There was however an almost continuous handrail (similar to the side rails), leading from near the starboard pump room entrance to near the foot of the starboard ladder to the forecastle deck (see Figure 9). In the conditions prevailing, any attempt to reach the forecastle head by this means would undoubtedly have involved personal risk. Nevertheless, the handrail was on the lee side of the deck and protected to some extent by the cargo pipework on the centreline. It must be considered a possibility that such an attempt, by competent seamen, could have been successful.

15.3   If this had been achieved or if people could have been put on the forecastle head by helicopter, it is not known what effects releasing the anchors might have had. When large tankers anchor, it is common to lower the anchor under power for a considerable way towards the bottom before releasing it. Very large tankers will usually lower the anchor all the way to the bottom under power. This practice is carried out to avoid an excessive build up of kinetic energy which cannot be absorbed by the brake. After she was abandoned by her crew, BRAER temporarily ceased drifting and was in about 50 metres of water over reasonable holding ground. If her anchors could have been released at that time, and the whole scope of the cables paid out under control, it is possible that they would have held the vessel. Or they might have acted as a drogue, taking hold later as she drifted into shallower depths of about 35 metres south-east of Horse Island. This can be no more than a possibility. (In a paper presented to a conference on mooring large vessels over 150,000 dwt at the Institute of Marine Engineers in 1979, the opinion was expressed that the anchoring equipment on such vessels was not designed to withstand emergency use in extreme weather conditions of more than Force 8).

15.4   Reference has been made earlier to the hawse pipes on BRAER being set at about 45° below the horizontal. This appears to be a sufficient angle to ensure, that if they had been released, the anchors would have 'run' under gravity from their housed positions. It is by no means unknown for anchors to fail to run from the hawse pipe when the windlass brake is released, the vertical component of the weight of the anchor not being enough to overcome the frictional resistance of the various parts of anchor and cable and the weight of the inner part of cable hanging in the cable locker. This cannot easily be anticipated because anchors are usually lowered outside the hawse pipe under power prior to being dropped. The frictional resistance of the anchor in the housed position will usually be greater if the hawse pipe is set at a smaller angle below the horizontal. It might therefore be worthwhile considering a need for changes to either Convention or class rule requirements, such that anchors are capable of ready release direct from the housed position, without the need for power.

15.5   A potential problem is that once released the cables might have 'taken charge', acquiring kinetic energy incapable of being absorbed by the brakes, and therefore running out to their full lengths. It is almost a certainty that if this happened both cables would have been lost, whether or not the ends had been secured in the chain lockers. There would also have been a high probability of fatal injuries to anyone in the vicinity. It would therefore have been difficult to control the dropping of the anchors unless it could have been done in short stages with careful handling of the brakes. In another of the papers to the Institute of Marine Engineers conference in 1979, dynamic braking systems for windlasses were discussed. It was envisaged that these would absorb kinetic energy, acquired either by the drifting vessel herself or by the anchors and cables as they are dropped. It is not known whether such systems have been developed and fitted to any large tankers.

15.6   The Inspectors have also considered whether large tankers should have a means by which seamen can safely reach the forecastle head from the accommodation to operate the anchors. A raised catwalk or 'flying bridge' with enclosed refuges at regular intervals, such as was common on smaller tankers, was considered. Another was that new tankers (which are required to be constructed with double sides) should have an enclosed passageway from aft to forward incorporated in the structure. This would require adequate lighting and a very efficient ventilation system. Both these solutions would incur considerable implementation costs. For new tankers, a relatively cheaper alternative would be to arrange the pipelines running forward to aft in such a way that there was a walkway at deck level with refuges at intervals. Some tankers are designed in this manner and they offer some protection to a person from seas sweeping across the deck. A further alternative, particularly for existing vessels, is a continuous handrail close to the fore and aft pipelines on both the port and starboard side. (BRAER had such a handrail but only on the starboard side.)

15.7   The possibility of releasing the anchors without the need to go forward has also been considered. Total remote control of anchoring operations in the offshore industry has already been developed and there have been classification society rules for such systems since 1989. These have been developed for use on semi-submersible units; the technology therefore exists to provide similar systems on large tankers. The emergency power required to operate the system, particularly on very large tankers, would be relatively high and for this reason a source of high pressure hydraulic power with a high reliability factor would probably be essential. An efficient 'fail safe' device would also be needed to avoid accidental releasing of the anchors during normal service.

16.   EMERGENCY TOWING ARRANGEMENTS FOR LARGE TANKERS

16.1   The only emergency towing arrangement traditionally provided on vessels for many years has been a heavy towing wire on a reel and a heavy shackle for connecting it to an anchor cable. The composite towline of wire and anchor cable, perhaps with the anchor still connected to additionally absorb sudden tensions, is an accepted method of towing another vessel at sea. The towing wire (often known as the 'insurance wire') could not usually be handled on a vessel without winch power and it is unlikely that it would be used anyway if the towing vessel was a tug with her own specialised towing equipment. Towing wires are not a Convention requirement and few vessels are now provided with them. If BRAER had been so equipped, it is highly unlikely that the wire could have been handled, due to the lack of winch power and the extreme weather conditions.

16.2   The investigation covered consideration of both developed systems and those at the planning stage aimed at assisting a tug to establish a tow with a disabled and possibly unmanned vessel. At least two tanker companies have equipped some of their vessels with various emergency arrangements. Some vessels only have a single towing wire on a reel whilst others, engaged in offshore loading, have pre-rigged towlines at the stern to pull them clear of the oil installation in an emergency. One of the companies has embarked on a programme to fit additional equipment to their vessels. This includes the provision of deck fittings to facilitate the setting up of a tow and the supply of nine-metre lengths of heavy chain cable, one at each end. The one at the stern will be permanently connected to a towing bracket. Neither operator has yet made provision for a 'rapid deployment system' to send a towline from a totally disabled vessel.

16.3   The publication 'Peril at Sea and Salvage - A Guide for Masters' was prepared by the International Chamber of Shipping and the Oil Companies International Marine Forum in 1979, following the AMOCO CADIZ accident. It has since been updated and expanded by the issue of two further editions; the latest one was issued in 1992. The Guide advises that helicopters have on occasions been used to assist in connecting towlines. In the case of BRAER this might have been a possibility, had there been more time in hand after the loss of the second rocket line fired from STAR SIRIUS.

The Guide also gives advice on the connecting of a tow to a vessel without power and some of it is very pertinent to the BRAER accident. A practical way of heaving a tug's towline to the vessel, using messengers and the tug's winch power, is explained. Had there been time, this method would have been preferable to heaving the lines from BRAER to STAR SIRIUS. In the event time was extremely limited and the plan suggested by STAR SIRIUS's Master was the right one in the circumstances.

65

16.4   Technical papers and various other sources, including several letters from members of the public, make it clear that there is no shortage of good practical ideas for the rapid deployment of a permanently attached towline from a disabled vessel. Where manual deployment from a tanker is necessary, it is best that it is done from the stern, where the crew are protected by the superstructure and the life-saving equipment is near at hand. The accommodation itself may also provide a 'safe haven' should one be needed. One such system, now being developed by a national oil company, incorporates a towing wire with a large thimble at the inner end and a lighter pennant at the outer end; the whole assembly is stowed within an oil-filled tube: between the after end of the tube and the ship's rail is a special fairlead into which the thimble locks; when deployed, the lighter pennant is passed through this fairlead to the tug by a messenger line; the tug then heaves the wire out of its container until the end thimble locks into the fairlead. An ex-submariner has described a permanently connected towline which, on a similar principle, is deployed by a lighter line; this system is used on submarines when it is hazardous to send crew on to the casing.

16.5   A paper in 'Seaways' (the journal of the Nautical Institute) proposed a way of setting up a tow which would withstand the sudden stresses experienced in heavy weather conditions. The proposal involved lowering the anchor and attaching the tug's towline to the cable. In the case of BRAER, the particular circumstances were not favourable for this method. If a landing had been made on the bow, the first priority would have been to try to drop both anchors to the bottom, hopefully with a successful outcome. Had STAR SIRIUS attempted to approach the bow to pass a messenger around the anchor cable there would have been a danger of collision due to the very heavy seas.

The same paper describes the work of a group of salvage specialists who have been working with Edinburgh University to develop a cost effective and practical tow connection system; this would enable a towline to be secured to an unmanned vessel, without the necessity of putting personnel on board.

16.6   Shortly after the BRAER accident a paper was submitted to the International Maritime Organization (IMO) for consideration by its Maritime Safety Committee. The paper contained details of a number of interim measures to protect the United Kingdom coast from accidental pollution. The measures included a voluntary code for laden tankers, which has since been published by the United Kingdom Chamber of Shipping. The Code makes wide ranging recommendations on operational matters as well as routeing. It stresses that the guidance in IMO Resolution A.535(13) on the provision of emergency towing equipment for tankers should be followed at the earliest opportunity.

Resolution A.535(13) was originally published in 1984. In the UK the attention of shipowners, shipbuilders, shiprepairers and salvors was drawn to A.535(13) by a Merchant Shipping Notice published by the Department of Transport later that year. The text of the Resolution was reproduced in full as an annex to the Notice, (see Annex 1). The recommendations are comprehensive and apply to tankers of more than 50,000 dwt built after 1984, which should be fitted with emergency towing arrangements at the bow and stern, and to tankers of more than 100,000 dwt built before 1984, which should be fitted with emergency towing positions at the bow and stern. (BRAER, having been built in 1975 and being 89,730 dwt, was in neither of these categories but was fitted with a 'bowstopper' on the centre line of the forecastle head; this would have been fitted primarily for use when the vessel loaded or discharged cargo at a single point mooring buoy but it can be used for attaching an emergency towing line). The recommended requirements include a capability to connect a tow in the absence of main power, and in particular the provision of fittings in the bow and the stern to facilitate the passing of a towing pennant from the assisting vessel, using the assisting vessel's power.

The IMO Sub-Committee on Ship Design and Equipment held its 36th session in February 1993. The agenda included a revision of Resolution A.535(13). It was agreed that the emergency towing arrangements for tankers, recommended to be fitted at each end, should be made mandatory and extended to apply to tankers of 20,000 dwt and above. The Sub-Committee also agreed that the provisions of the Resolution could be improved so that emergency towing equipment would be pre-rigged and capable of being rapidly deployed. Arrangements were put in hand for the drafting of an amendment to the 1974 SOLAS Convention and a review of the towing requirements in the Resolution.

The draft text of amendments to Chapter V of the Convention was approved by the Sub-Committee (see Annex 2). On appraisal it was found that a significant revision of the Resolution would be needed to incorporate rapid deployment and towing line retrieval capability; such a task could not be completed within the time available for the 36th Session of the Sub-Committee. It was therefore recommended that the Navigation Sub-Committee be requested to review and revise the Resolution, where appropriate, with a high priority.

16.7   Any requirements for emergency towing arrangements on tankers need to be agreed internationally. It serves no purpose for an administration to act unilaterally as safety of life at sea and protection of the environment is a major international issue. It is welcomed that IMO is treating this matter with urgency and it is hoped the outcome may prevent a similar disaster to that of BRAER occurring in the future.

17.   OTHER MEASURES TO AVOID TANKER ACCIDENTS

17.1   In the aftermath of BRAER a number of other measures have been taken to avoid tanker accidents around the United Kingdom coast. The Shetland Islands Conference on Managing the Marine Environment was opened by the Minister of State for Shipping in March 1993. The Conference was told about the actions on both national and international levels being taken to avoid similar accidents in the future. The best known of these was the Government's decision to set up an independent Inquiry, chaired by The Right Honourable The Lord Donaldson of Lymington:

> "To advise on whether any further measures are appropriate and feasible to protect the UK coastline from pollution from merchant shipping. Due consideration should be given to the international and economic implications of any new measures."

17.2   Another measure taken by the Government was to convene a meeting of national and international organisations responsible for worldwide tanker operations. The main purpose of the meeting was to look in to possible interim measures and recommendations that could be put in place for tankers using United Kingdom waters, to protect sensitive areas from the risk of accident and consequent pollution. The United Kingdom industry, through the Chamber of Shipping, took the initiative and were invited to prepare a voluntary code. Routeing provisions based on the Code (with some minor changes) were submitted by the Government to IMO and adopted by them in November 1993.

The Code, titled 'Interim Voluntary Code - Routeing in UK waters for Ships carrying Oil and other Hazardous Cargoes in Bulk' has been referred to in the previous section of this Report. It recommends measures whereby shipowners and shipmasters can reduce the risk of pollution caused by collision or grounding around the UK coast. Matters which are addressed include the testing of vessels' essential systems, passage planning, compliance with existing routeing schemes and voluntary reporting schemes, precautions in case of breakdown and the summoning of salvage assistance without delay. The Code reviews routeing arrangements and practices in sensitive areas and makes recommendations on their use by laden tankers.

The Fair Isle Straits are one of the sensitive areas for which new measures have been adopted. IMO have recommended that all laden tankers intending to use the Straits should report their movements to Shetland Coastguard. Detailed recommended routes through North or South Fair Isle Channels will come into force once the necessary hydrographic survey work has been completed, probably in 1994. IMO has also introduced new 'Areas to be Avoided' around Fair Isle and Orkney and extended the existing 'Area to be Avoided' off the Shetland Islands.

17.3   Another issue of concern is the availability of suitable tugs around the UK coast, in the light of the decline in recent years of the UK towage and salvage industry. The Government has commissioned a survey to establish the availability of salvage resources to assist a disabled tanker off the coast of the United Kingdom. The results of the survey have been made available to Lord Donaldson's Inquiry.

17.4   Internationally, the new IMO Regulations relating to the construction of oil tankers will contribute significantly to the prevention of pollution. Within Europe, other measures include changes to Port State Control procedures within the Paris Memorandum of Understanding. Changes to vessel inspection procedures put an emphasis on operational matters and the 'targeting' of vessels which are on the registers of flag states with poor safety records. Further efforts are being made in this direction by IMO, which has recently convened a Sub-Committee to examine measures which can be taken to ensure that member states implement and enforce Conventions which they have ratified.

PART IV   CONCLUSION

18.   FINDINGS

The Inquiry carried out by the Inspectors has covered great detail. It is unfortunate that they were never able to get on board BRAER but they received complete co-operation from the owners of sister ships to BRAER and from many others. In particular the Inspectors received the full co-operation of the flag state of the vessel; the Liberian Authorities carried out an investigation of their own in parallel with the Inspector's Inquiry.

The Inquiry only covered the period up to the time the vessel went aground: it did not cover the pollution and its aftermath which was the subject of separate inquiries by other Government bodies.

To reach their findings the Inspectors had to rely to some extent on supposition, but this was consistent with good, unbiased investigatory work. I consider that the findings given in this section of the Report are a true reflection of the actual events which occurred and I support their conclusions.

The main findings of this Inquiry are as follows:

18.1   The stopping of the main engine at approximately 0440 hrs on 5 January, followed shortly afterwards by the loss of all main electrical power, was due to serious sea water contamination of the common diesel oil supply to both main engine and generator.

18.2   The initial contamination occurred after the entry of sea water to the port double bottom diesel oil storage tank. The sea water entered the tank from the upper deck through the damaged after air pipe to the tank. During the subsequent topping up of the diesel oil settling tank on the 2000 hrs to 2400 hrs watch on the evening of 4 January, an indeterminate amount of water would have been transferred from the double bottom tank to the settling tank.

18.3   The damage to the after air pipe of the port double bottom diesel oil tank was caused by one or more of the spare steel pipe sections which had broken adrift on deck sometime during the morning of 4 January, when the vessel was rolling heavily in a severe southerly gale and frequently shipping water on deck.

18.4   A second source of direct sea water contamination to both settling and service diesel oil tanks, was probably from the starboard side of the upper deck, by way of the common air pipe to those tanks. It is not possible to say when water first gained entry by this means. It may be that the initial failure of the air pipe was sometime during the late evening of 4 January, followed by a second and more serious failure around 0400 hrs on 5 January.

18.5   The failure of the air pipe to the diesel oil settling and service tanks was probably due to damage at deck level, adjacent to the deck penetration piece. This would have been caused by the loose pipe sections, one of which is known to have been on the starboard side of the deck. Alternatively, the float valve in the head of the air pipe was damaged either by the loose pipe sections or at some time prior to the final voyage.

18.6   When it was reported to the Master on the morning of 4 January that the pipe sections had broken loose he failed to take any action to try to have them re-secured or jettisoned or simply to observe them to see the damage they may have been causing. This was a serious dereliction of the Master's duty to preserve the seaworthiness of his vessel and the safety of her crew. The danger that these loose pipes posed to the integrity of the fuel tank air pipes was not appreciated by him or by anybody else on board, either at this time or later.

18.7   The Superintendent, the Chief Engineer, the senior Assistant Engineers and also the Master failed to realise the cause of the sea water contamination. In particular, an earlier intervention by the Superintendent and an analytical approach by him might have resulted in discovery of the source of the water entry.

18.8   The repairs to the control system of the auxiliary boiler, the resultant lowering of steam pressure and the changing of the main engine operation from heavy fuel oil to diesel oil all fell within normal watchkeeping duties. The failure of the boiler to re-ignite was due to the presence of sea water contamination in the boiler supply line from the diesel oil settling tank.

18.9   Towage assistance was requested by the Master at 0526 hrs, approximately 45 minutes after the loss of power. It was not possible for towage assistance to be given to BRAER before the decision to abandon her was made three hours later. That decision was a correct one, as the vessel was by that time in imminent danger of grounding.

18.10   Access to the anchors by the crew of BRAER, prior to the abandonment, posed a risk due to the extreme weather conditions. However, a safety rail was fitted on the lee side of the deck and access could have been successfully accomplished, if it had been attempted by competent seamen.

18.11   It was not possible to land personnel on the forecastle head of BRAER to release her anchors; the close proximity of her foremast posed a risk to safe helicopter operations.

         Further findings are as follows:

18.12   BRAER had valid Convention Certificates when she sailed from Mongstad on 3 January 1993. At that time she was structurally sound with no known significant deficiencies.

18.13   The Master and Officers held valid Licences of Competence issued by the Republic of Liberia, the flag state authority.

18.14   The route as planned was a normal route, commonly followed.

18.15   The securing arrangements of the spare steel pipe sections carried on deck, although they failed, had proved to be adequate during previous Atlantic crossings in adverse weather.

18.16   The condition of the machinery, according to the available evidence, suggests that although a back log of repair and maintenance work had built up, this was being rectified by the use of 'riding crews' and organised off hire repair periods. There was no evidence of neglect or lack of maintenance.

18.17   During the passage from Mongstad, the Master was at fault in allowing the navigation officers and ratings to spend their entire periods of bridge duty inside the wheelhouse. This was an unseamanlike practice, particularly in heavy weather conditions when it was essential to be aware of what was happening on deck areas not within sight of the wheelhouse. Checks of most of the outside deck areas aft could have been made from the bridge and captain's deck or from within the accommodation, with no risk to crew safety. Had this been done, the breaking loose of the spare pipes might have been noticed earlier.

18.18   The Master's decision to make for a sheltered anchorage in the Moray Firth was the right one, on the advice given to him. He did not call for a tug as soon as the power failure occurred because BRAER was at that time in open water and he believed that power could be restored under the direction of the Superintendent, a highly qualified and experienced marine engineer.

18.19   The Master's decision to request towage assistance at 0526 hrs was the correct one. However, he should have supplemented his request to Coastguard with a request for towage to 'all stations', using the appropriate Urgency prefixes.

18.20   The Master made no effort to ascertain the direction and rate of drift of his vessel, even after being asked to do so by Coastguard. Means to do this were available to him.

18.21   The decision to evacuate non-essential crew was timely and correct.

18.22   The Superintendent, the Engineers and the ratings who remained in the engine room of BRAER to continue efforts to restore power until the last possible moment did so with little regard for their own safety.

18.23   Shetland Coastguard failed to relay the Master's request for towage assistance as soon as possible and by all available means; the telephone calls they made after his initial request lacked urgency. However, even if the available tugs had been despatched with the minimum of delay, none of them could have reached BRAER before the final abandonment commenced.

18.24   BRAER did not ground as soon as had been expected because an outflow of water from West Voe, set up by the severe onshore gales, halted the vessel's drift and set her to the south and into the wind. She was then set to the west and passed Horse Island by the west going tidal stream. Once past Horse Island BRAER was again predominantly influenced by the southerly gale and drifted in a north by west direction until she finally grounded on the west side of Garths Ness.

18.25   Shetland Coastguard were not given a clear and urgent mandate to plan and organise efforts to avoid the grounding of BRAER, after her abandonment. In particular, with the tug STAR SIRIUS on the way, there should have been early contingency planning to prepare for her arrival. This was needed in parallel with the planning which was made to attempt to land volunteers at the forward end of the vessel to release the anchors. However, there is no evidence that the lack of this forward planning contributed to the grounding.

18.26   The co-ordination of the evacuation of the crew from BRAER was competently organised. The crews of Rescue Helicopters 117 and 137 carried out their duties in a most exemplary manner in very adverse and dangerous conditions. The evacuation of all the crew of BRAER without injury was carried out competently and with great skill, as was the landing and evacuation of the volunteers.

18.27   The Master and crew of STAR SIRIUS displayed excellent seamanship and did all that they possibly could to establish a tow.

18.28   The tugs SWAABIE and TIRRICK and the Lerwick Lifeboat put out to sea without hesitation when asked to do so. This was in the best traditions of the sea.

18.29   Those who volunteered to return to BRAER, especially the four who were landed on the stern, displayed bravery and determination in a very dangerous situation.

19.   RECOMMENDATIONS

The accident highlights a number of lessons to be learnt which are self evident. The immediate cause of the accident was the contamination of the diesel fuel supply by seawater entering the storage tanks from damaged air pipes. The principal cause of that damage was the failure of those on board to ensure that corrective action was taken when it was known that the spare pipes, which were stowed on the upper deck aft, had broken loose. This was a matter of seamanship and to those on board, with their seagoing experience, it should have been obvious that the loose pipes presented a hazard unless some action was taken. It should have been apparent that the integrity of the fuel oil system was being placed in jeopardy by the loose pipes hitting the air pipes on the port side of the vessel. It has not been possible to say with any degree of certainty whether the entry of water into the diesel oil settling and service tanks via the common air pipe was due to damage to that pipe or a defective float seal valve head. The importance of these valves and the need to ensure that they are operational and efficient at all times should not be under-estimated.

Apart from the lessons to be learnt, the Inquiry into the accident and the findings of the Inspectors also lead to a number of recommendations being made. If implemented, these recommendations should prevent recurrence of such an accident and generally improve safety of life at sea and the protection of the environment. In making these recommendations cognizance is taken of the actions already taken or being taken internationally through the International Maritime Organization (IMO) and on a more national level in the UK. These actions are referred to in this Report.

The recommendations made are as follows:

1.   The Marine Directorate of the Department of Transport should, through the International Maritime Organization (IMO), seek to ensure that the revision and strengthening of the Standards of Training, Certification and Watchkeeping Convention (STCW), now in hand under an accelerated procedure, lays stress on the need for practical experience, training and thorough assessment of competence in seamanship in the widest sense of the term. Flag States accepting the certificates of other Administrations should take care to ensure that these matters have been properly addressed.

2.   The provisions of the International Management Code for the Safe Operation of Ships and for Pollution Prevention (the International Safety Management (ISM) Code) recently adopted by the International Maritime Organization (IMO) should be implemented by the shore management of shipping companies as a matter of urgency before they become mandatory. The International Chamber of Shipping (ICS) and the International Shipping Federation (ISF), who have published guidelines on the application of the Code, should encourage implementation by their members by every means possible.

3.   The Marine Directorate of the Department of Transport should undertake research on the feasibility of methods enabling the controlled and safe lowering of the anchors from the housed position into deep water to the full scope of the anchor cables and without the need for power. If any methods are considered feasible a requirement for fitting them should be pursued through the International Maritime Organization (IMO).

4.   The Marine Directorate of the Department of Transport should, through the International Maritime Organization (IMO), seek to ensure, that the revision of Resolution A.535(13) (Provision of Emergency Towing Equipment for Tankers) currently underway also incorporates provisions for safe access to the anchors from the after superstructure of tankers. The Maritime Safety Committee of IMO should be urged to give urgent priority to the completion of the review and revision of the Resolution, with a view to making the requirements mandatory by an amendment to Chapter V of the 1974 SOLAS Convention.

5.   The Marine Directorate of the Department of Transport should ensure that HM Coastguard, on receipt of a request for towage assistance from any vessel carrying petroleum or dangerous cargo, relay and promulgate the request immediately by all means of communication. This action should be taken whether or not the vessel has declared an Urgency situation.

6.   The Marine Directorate of the Department of Transport should take the necessary steps to allow the intervention powers of the Secretary of State for Transport under the Prevention of Oil Pollution Act 1971, which are delegated to the Director Marine Emergencies Organisation (DMEO) alone, to be delegated further. This should be two-fold. Firstly they should be delegated to the DMEO's deputy to allow for circumstances when the DMEO is not available. Secondly the DMEO, or in his absence his deputy, should be able to delegate the powers to a senior officer of the Department of Transport located in the area of the incident when local knowledge might result in a faster response to the emergency.

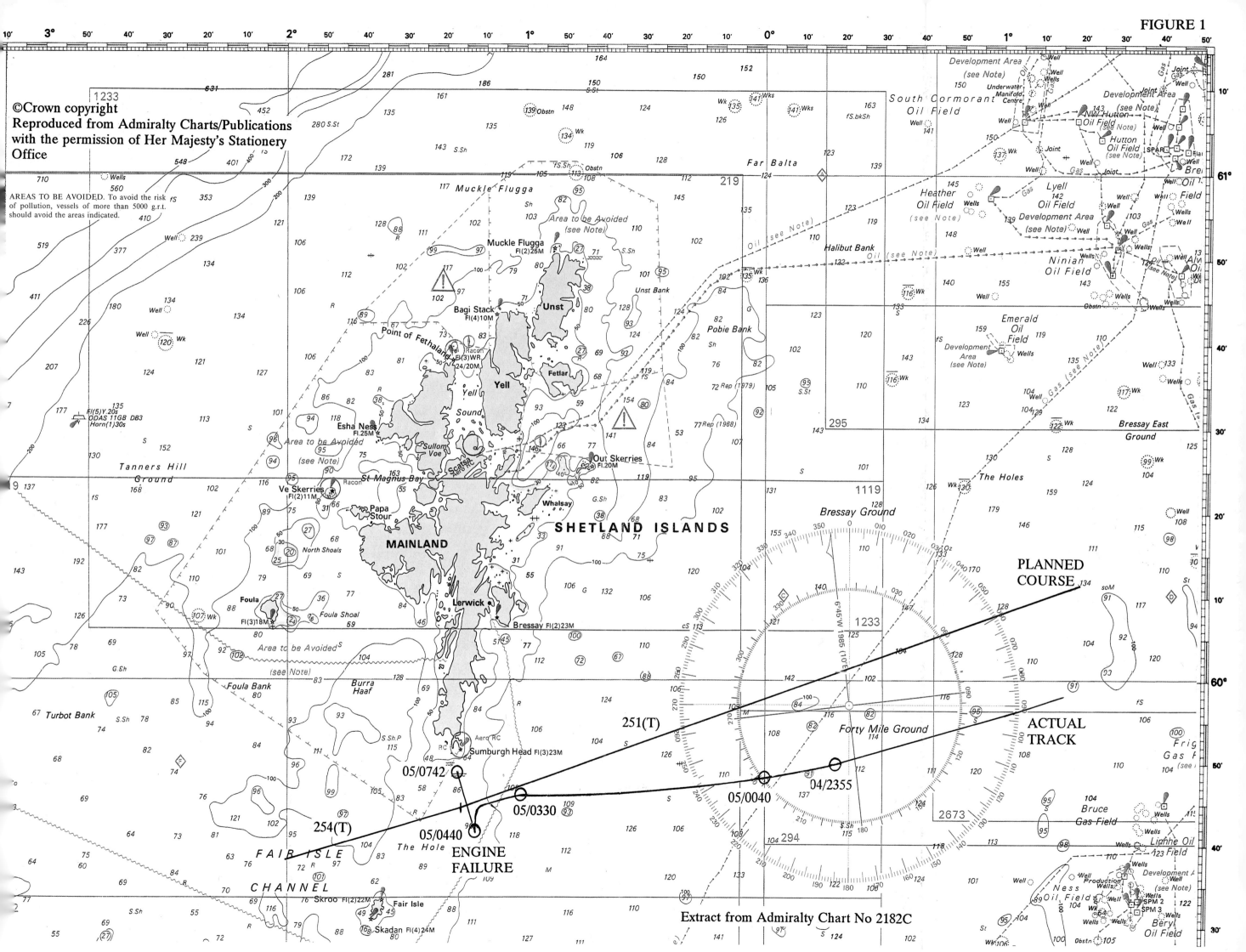

FIGURE 1

©Crown copyright
Reproduced from Admiralty Charts/Publications
with the permission of Her Majesty's Stationery
Office

AREAS TO BE AVOIDED. To avoid the risk
of pollution, vessels of more than 5000 g.r.t.
should avoid the areas indicated.

SHETLAND ISLANDS

MAINLAND

PLANNED
COURSE

ACTUAL
TRACK

251(T)

254(T)

05/0742

05/0330

05/0440
ENGINE
FAILURE

05/0040

04/2355

FAIR ISLE

CHANNEL

Extract from Admiralty Chart No 2182C

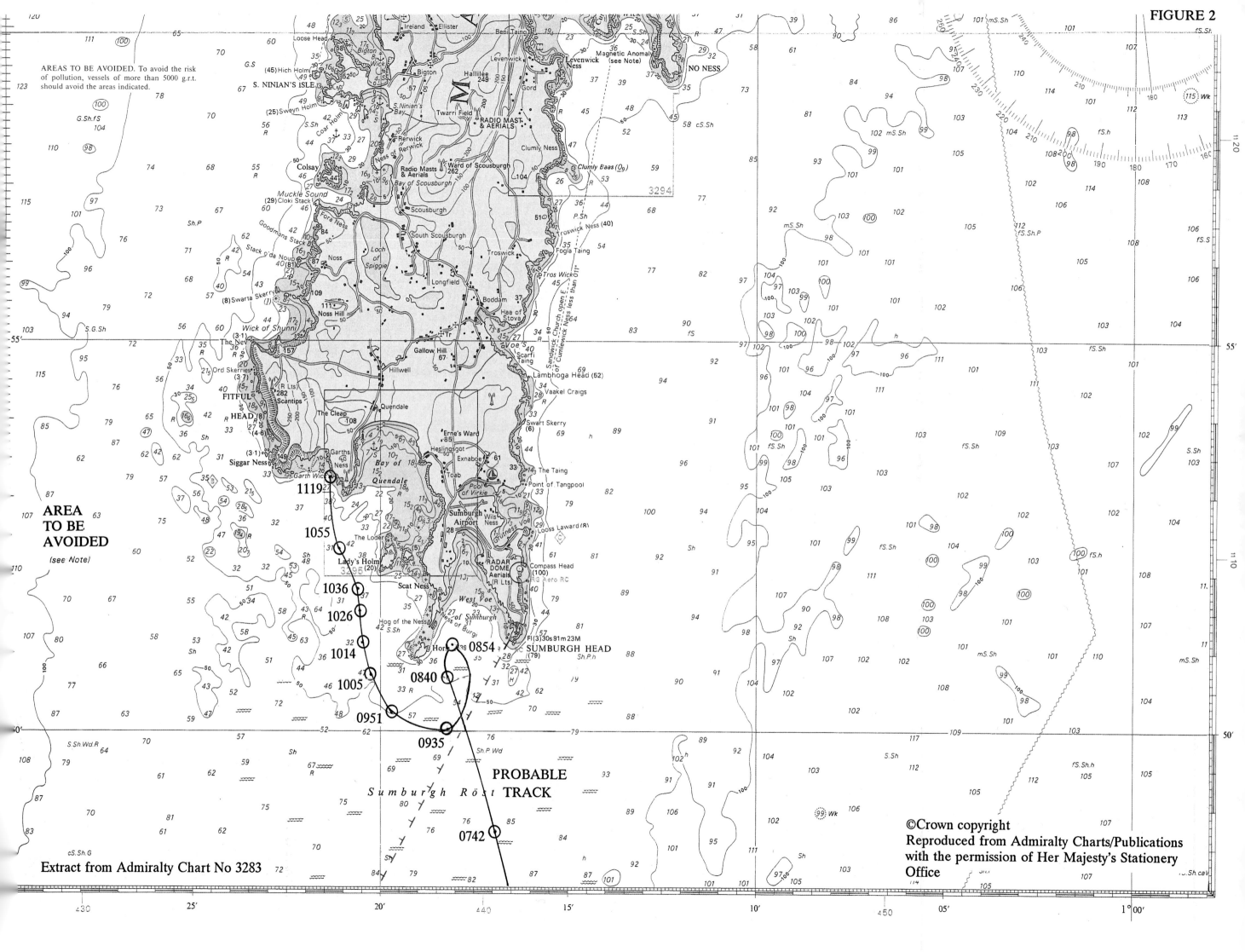

FIGURE 2

FIGURE 3

Photograph courtesy of RAF Lossiemouth

BRAER aground showing loose pipes,
port and starboard sides aft

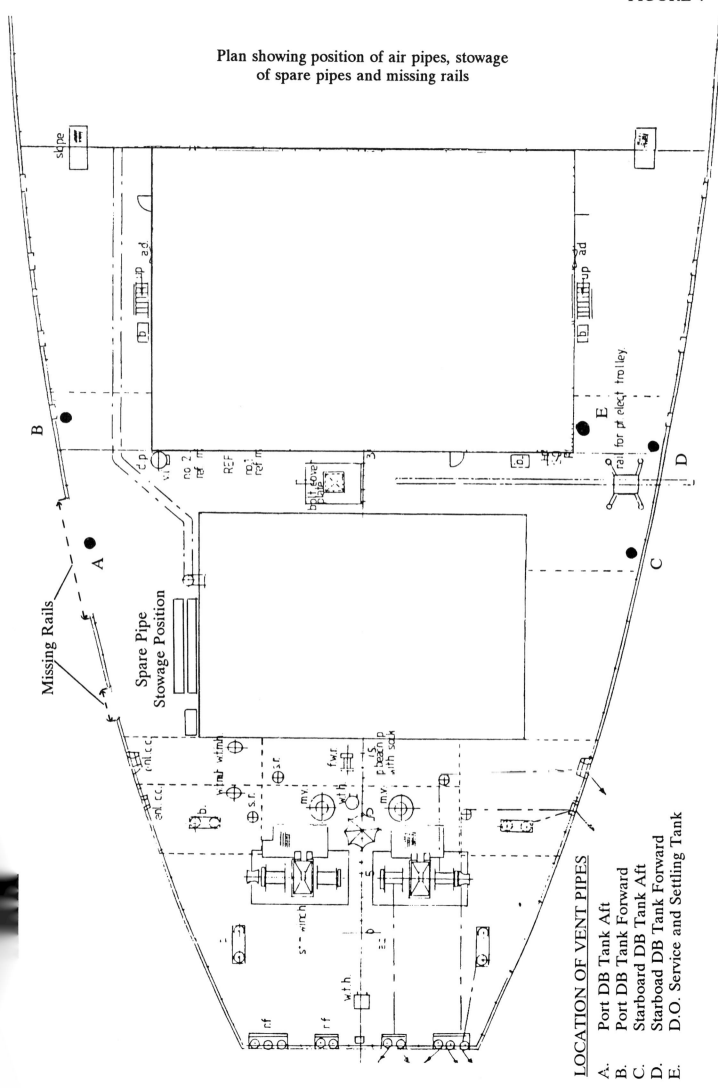

FIGURE 4

Plan showing position of air pipes, stowage
of spare pipes and missing rails

LOCATION OF VENT PIPES

A.   Port DB Tank Aft
B.   Port DB Tank Forward
C.   Starboard DB Tank Aft
D.   Starboad DB Tank Forward
E.   D.O. Service and Settling Tank

FIGURE 5

Photograph courtesy of Vine Abel & Co. Singapore Pte Ltd

Photograph courtesy of the Marine Department, Republic of Singapore

Port double bottom diesel oil tank, aft air pipe
(Photographs taken on sister ships)

FIGURE 6

Photograph courtesy of RAF Lossiemouth

BRAER aground showing broken rails port side aft in way of air pipes

FIGURE 7

Photograph courtesy of Vine Abel & Co. Singapore Pte Ltd

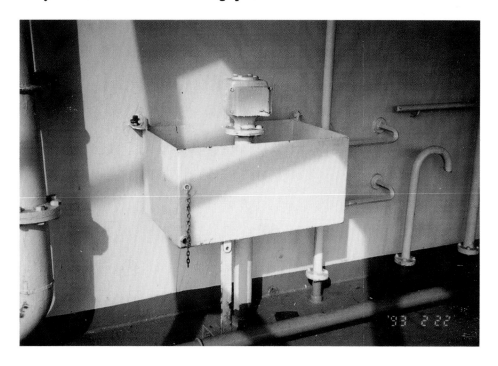

Photograph courtesy of the Marine Department, Republic of Singapore

Common air pipe to diesel oil settling and
service tanks, starboard side upper deck
(Photographs taken on two sister ships)

FIGURE 8

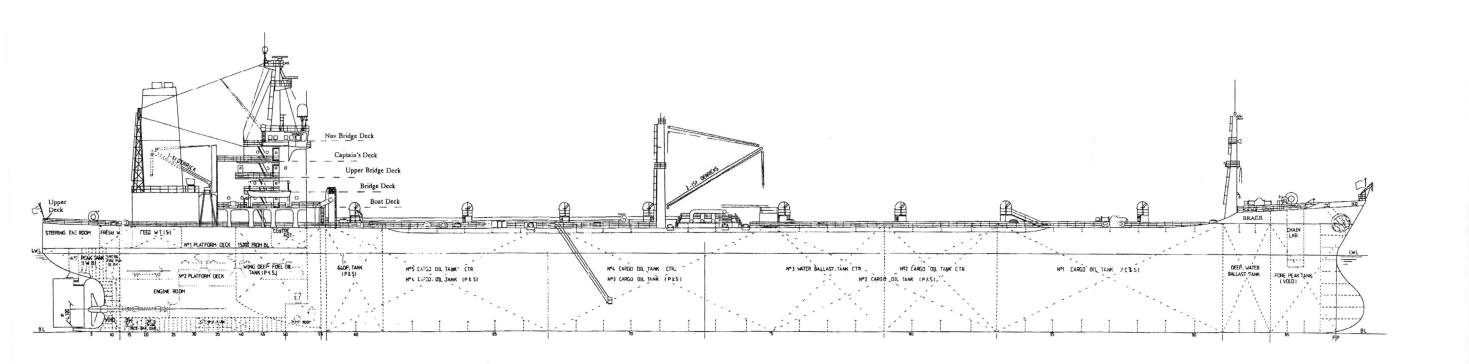

General arrangement "BRAER"

FIGURE 9

View of upper deck looking forward, taken on sister ship

ANNEX I

IMO

RESOLUTION A535(13)

adopted on 17 November 1983

RECOMMENDATION ON EMERGENCY TOWING REQUIREMENTS FOR TANKERS

THE ASSEMBLY,

RECALLING Article 16(j) of the Convention of the International Maritime Organization concerning the functions of the Assembly in relation to regulations concerning maritime safety,

NOTING that ships carrying oil, liquefied gases or other hazardous liquids in bulk (referred to hereinafter as tankers), in emergencies such as complete mechanical breakdowns, may need to be towed out of danger,

RECOGNIZING that some existing tankers are equipped with special fittings for use at single-point moorings which may be suitable for emergency towing.

HAVING CONSIDERED the recommendation made by the Maritime Safety Committee at its forty eighth session,

1.   ADOPTS the Recommendation on Emergency Towing Requirements for Tankers, the text of which is set out in the Annex to this resolution;

2.   RECOMMENDS that all Governments concerned take appropriate steps to give effect to the Recommendation as soon as possible;

3.   REQUESTS the Maritime Safety Committee to keep the Recommendation under review, in particular in respect to new towing concepts which may be introduced and to report as necessary to the Assembly.

RECOMMENDATION ON EMERGENCY TOWING REQUIREMENTS FOR TANKERS

1.   Purpose

The purpose of this Recommendation is to facilitate salvage and emergency towing operations on new and existing tankers primarily to reduce the risk of pollution. The Recommendation recognizes the need for harmonization of components in the towing system and uses as a reference the system shown in Figure 1. The major components of the system are the tug or towing vessel; the towline; the pennant; the chafing chain; the fairlead and the towing gear connection or strongpoint on the vessel to be towed. The system should facilitate ease of connections and should be capable of being connected and released on board the towed vessel in the absence of main power. The system should be standardized at the point of connection of the towline to the chafing chain.

2.   REQUIREMENTS

2.1   Application

All tankers greater than 50,000 tonnes deadweight built after adoption of this resolution should be fitted with emergency towing arrangements at the bow and stern. All tankers greater than 100,000 tonnes deadweight built before adoption, should be fitted with emergency towing positions at the bow and stern at the first scheduled drydocking following adoption but not later than five years after adoption. Each towing position should be fitted with a strongpoint, chafing chain and fairlead.

2.2   Strength of Towing System Components

Towing system components (strongpoint, chafing chain, fairlead and supporting structure) should have a working strength of at least 2000 kN (working strength is defined as one half ultimate strength). The strength should be sufficient for all angles of towline up to 90 ° from the ship's centreline.

2.3   Location of Strongpoint and Fairlead

The bow and stern strongpoint and fairleads should be located so as to facilitate towing from either side of the bow or stern and minimize the stress on the towing system. The axis of the towing gear should, as far as practicable, be parallel to and not more than 1.5 m from either side of the centreline. The distance between the strongpoint and the fairlead should be not less than 2.7 m and not more than 5 m.

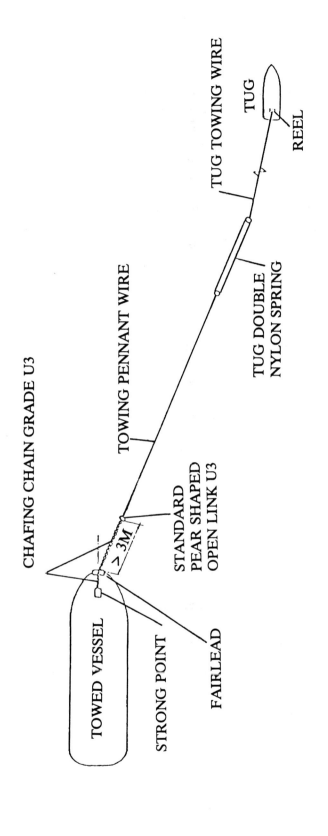

CHAFING CHAIN GRADE U3

TOWING PENNANT WIRE

TUG TOWING WIRE

TUG

REEL

TUG DOUBLE
NYLON SPRING

> 3M

STANDARD
PEAR SHAPED
OPEN LINK U3

TOWED VESSEL

STRONG POINT

FAIRLEAD

FIGURE 1. EXAMPLE OF TANKER TOWED FROM THE BOW

2.4 Strongpoint

The towing connection should be a stopper or bracket or other fitting of equivalent strength and ease of connection to the satisfaction of the Administration.

2.5 Fairleads

.1 *Size* Fairleads should have an opening large enough to pass the largest portion of the chafing chain, towing pennant or their connections. The minimum opening should be an oval with horizontal axis of at least 600 mm and vertical axis of 450 mm.

.2 *Type* Fairleads should be constructed so that the chafing chain will be constrained within the fairlead during the towing operation.

.3 *Geometry* Fairleads should be configured to avoid the risk of fouling when a strain is taken on the chain and to minimize the reduction in strength of the chafing chain when the chain is at 90° angle to the fairlead. The ratio of the fairlead chain bearing surface diameter to chain diameter should be at least 7:1. The outboard lips of the fairleads should as far as practicable be flush with the bulwarks. The inboard end of the fairlead should be fitted to avoid fouling of any part of the towing system when under load or being handled.

.4 *Vertical location* The fairleads should be located as close as possible to the deck and, in any case, in such a position that the chafing chain is approximately parallel to the deck when it is under strain between the strongpoint and the fairlead.

2.6 Chafing Chain

.1 *Stowage* The chafing chain should be stowed in such a way as to be rapidly connected to the strongpoint.

.2 *Length* The chafing chain should be long enough to ensure that the towing pennant remains outside the fairlead during the towing operation. A chain extending from the strongpoint to a point at least 3 m beyond the fairlead should meet this criterion.

.3 *Construction* The chafing chain should be 76 mm in diameter, grade U-3, stud link chain.

.4 *Connecting links* One end of the chafing chain should be suitable for connection to the strongpoint. The other end should be fitted with a standardized pear-shaped open link with the dimensions shown in Figure 2. Connecting links should be constructed of grade U-3 steel.

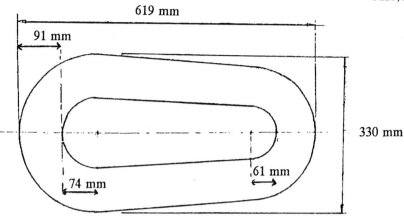

Figure 2. Standardised pear shaped link

2.7 Fittings for Connection

Tankers should be fitted in the bow and stern with suitable fittings which facilitate passing the towing pennant from the rescue vessel using the rescue vessel's power.

3. INFORMATION TO BE AVAILABLE FOR A TOWING VESSEL

3.1 Any ship requiring towing assistance should have available on board information concerning emergency towing arrangements at the bow and stern. A standard list of such information is given in the appendix to this Recommendation.

3.2 This information should be displayed permanently on the navigating bridge or be otherwise readily available for immediate transmission to the towing vessel.

4. EXISTING TANKERS

When considering the requirements in paragraph 2 for tankers greater than 100,000 tonnes deadweight built before adoption of this Recommendation, the Administration should take into account existing fittings and arrangements and permit their use wherever reasonable and practicable. Notwithstanding the above, the requirements in paragraph 2.6.4 should be maintained.

LIST OF INFORMATION TO BE TRANSMITTED TO THE TOWING SHIP

1.   **USABLE STRONGPOINTS**

Type
Dimensions
Working strength in tonnes (one half ultimate strength).

1.1   **For a Stopper**

Maximum and minimum size of chain accepted.

1.2   **For a Towing Bracket**

Clearance width between side plates
Length and thickness of towing bracket pin
Clear distance between pin and base plate
Distance between back of pin and front of side plates.

1.3   **For Bitts (Ships not Fitted with Special Strongpoint)**

Diameter of bitts
Possibility of using two pairs of bitts simultaneously
Working strength in tonnes (one-half ultimate strength).

2.   **FAIRLEADS**

Type
Internal dimensions (dimensions of horizontal and vertical axes)
Distance between fairlead and strongpoint
Position in relation to ship's centreline and deck.

3.   **OTHER COMPONENTS AVAILABLE ON BOARD**

3.1   **Existence of a Chafing Chain**

Diameter
Length
Strength

3.3   **Other Components, if any**

Possibility of using ship's winches in order to haul a towing wire on board.

DRAFT AMENDMENTS TO SOLAS CHAPTER V ON EMERGENCY TOWING ARRANGEMENTS ON TANKERS

1   Add new regulation V/15-1 as follows:

"Regulation 15-1

Emergency Towing Arrangements on Tankers

An emergency towing arrangement shall be fitted at both ends on board all tankers of 20,000 dwt and above constructed on or after [1 January 1996]. For tankers constructed before [1 January 1996] such an arrangement shall be fitted at the first scheduled dry-docking after [1 January 1996], but not later than, [1 January 1999]. The design and construction of the towing arrangements shall be approved by the Administration, based on guidelines developed by the Organization*."

---

*   Refer to the Guidelines on Emergency Towing Arrangements for Tankers to be developed by the Organization.